MW01103862

Islam and Human Rights

Muhammad Zafrulla Khan

ISLAM INTERNATIONAL PUBLICATIONS LIMITED

ISLAM AND HUMAN RIGHTS

by Sir Muhammad Zafrulla Khan

First published in 1967
Several editions published from 1976 to 2016
Present edition published in England in 2016

Published by
Islam International Publications Ltd
(Additional Wakaalat-e-Tasneef, UK)
Islamabad, Sheephatch Lane
Tilford, Surrey
GU10 2AQ United Kingdom

Cover Design: Salman Sajid

Printed and bound by
CPI Group (UK) Ltd,
Croydon, CR0 4YY

ISBN: 978-1-84880-862-1

MUHAMMAD ZAFRULLA KHAN

Muhammad Zafrulla Khan was distinguished not only as an expounder of Islam but as a leader in public life. He was an eminent scholar in the field of comparative religion. He was appointed Foreign Minister of Pakistan in 1947; for many years he led the Pakistan Delegation to the General Assembly of the United Nations, and he was President of the General Assembly's Seventeenth Session. Since then he has served as Judge and President of the International Court of Justice at the Hague. He is the author of a number of books about Islam and about its comparison with other faiths.

Contents

Islam and Human Rights

The Universal Declaration of Human Rights adopted by the General Assembly of the United Nation on December 10, 1948 embodies the broadest consensus of contemporary civilisation on the subject of Human Rights. This booklet attempts a comparative study of Islam and The Declaration. The presentation of Islamic values is based almost entirely upon the Holy Quran and the Sunnah of the Holy Prophet of Islam, the two most authentic and authoritative sources available for the purpose. The references to the Holy Quran are cited in the text; all other references are added in the footnotes.

To assist the reader towards a fuller comprehension of the main thesis the Introductory Chapter is followed by a brief outline of Islamic teachings on man and the Universe, Social values and Economic values.

Zafrulla Khan
The Hague,
July, 1967.

Universal Declaration of Human Rights

ON DECEMBER 10, 1948, the General Assembly of the United Nations adopted and proclaimed the Universal Declaration of Human Rights, the full text of which appears in the following pages. Following the historic act the Assembly called upon all Member countries to publicize the text of the Declaration and "to cause it to be disseminated, displayed, read and expounded principally in schools and other educational institutions, without distinction based on the political status of countries or territories."

PREAMBLE

Universal Declaration of Human Rights

WHEREAS recognition of the inherent dignity and of the equal and inalienable rights of all members of the human family is the foundation of freedom, justice and peace in the world,

WHEREAS disregard of and contempt for human rights have resulted in barbarous acts which have outraged the conscience of mankind, and the advent of a world in which human beings shall enjoy freedom of speech and belief in freedom from fear and want has been proclaimed as the highest aspiration of the common people,

WHEREAS is is essential, if man is not to be compelled to have recourse, as a last resort, to rebellion against tyranny and oppression, that human rights should be protected by the rule of law,

WHEREAS it is essential to promote the development of friendly relations between nations,

WHEREAS the people of the United Nations have in the Charter reaffirmed their faith in fundamental human rights, in the dignity and worth of the human person and in the equal rights of men and women and have determined to promote social progress and better standards of life in larger freedom,

WHEREAS Member States have pledged themselves to achieve, in co-operation with the United Nations, the promotion of universal respect for and observance of human rights and fundamental freedoms,

WHEREAS a common understanding of these rights and freedoms is of the greatest importance for the full realization of this pledge.

Now, Therefore,

THE GENERAL ASSEMBLY

proclaims

THIS UNIVERSAL DECLARATION OF HUMAN RIGHTS as a common standard of achievement for all peoples and all nations, to the end that every individual and every organ of society, keeping this Declaration constantly in mind, shall strive by teaching and education to promote respect for these rights and freedoms and by progressive measures, national and international, to secure their universal and effective recognition and observance, both among the peoples of Member States themselves and among the peoples of territories under their jurisdiction.

Article 1. All human beings are born free and equal in dignity and rights. They are endowed with reason and conscience and should act towards one another in a spirit of brotherhood.

Article 2. Everyone is entitled to all the rights and freedoms set forth in this Declaration, without distinction of any kind, such as race, colour, sex, language, religion, political or other opinion, national or social origin, property, birth or other status.

Futhermore, no distinction shall be made on the basis of the political, jurisdictional or international status of the country or territory to which a person belongs, whether it be independent, trust, non-self-governing or under any other limitations of sovereignty.

Article 3. Everyone has the right to life, liberty and security of person.

Article 4. No one shall be held in slavery or servitude; slavery and the slave trade shall be prohibited in all their forms.

Article 5. No one shall be subjected to torture or to cruel, inhuman or degrading treatment or punishment.

Article 6. Everyone has the right to recognition everywhere as a person before the law.

Article 7. All are equal before the law and are entitled without any discrimination to equal protection of the law. All are entitled to equal protection against any discrimination in violation of this Declaration and against any incitement to such discrimination.

Article 8. Everyone has the right to an effective remedy by the competent national tribunals for acts violating the fundamental rights granted him by the constitution or by law.

Ariticle 9. No one shall be subjected to arbitrary arrest, detention or exile.

Article 10. Everyone is entitled in full equality to a fair and public hearing by an independent and impartial tribunal, in the determination of his rights and obligations and of any criminal charge against him.

Article 11. (1) Everyone charged with a penal offence has the right to be presumed innocent until proved guilty according to law in a public trial at which he has had all the guarantees necessary for his defence.

(2) No one shall be held guilty of any penal offence on account of any act or omission which did not constitute a penal offence, under national or international law, at the time when it was committed. Nor shall a heavier penalty be imposed than the one that was applicable at the time the penal offence was committed.

Article 12. No one shall be subjected to arbitrary interference with his privacy, family, home or correspondence, nor to attacks upon his honour and reputation. Everyone has the right to the protection of the law against such interference or attacks.

Article 13. (1) Everyone has the right to freedom of movement and residence within the borders of each state.

(2) Everyone has the right to leave any country, including his own, and to return to his country.

Article 14. (1) Everyone has the right to seek and to enjoy in other countries asylum from persecution.

(2) This right may not be invoked in the case of prosecutions genuinely arising from non-political crimes or from acts contrary to the purposes and principles of the United Nations.

Article 15. (1) Everyone has the right to a nationality.

(2) No one shall be arbitrarily deprived of his nationality nor denied the right to change his nationality.

Article 16. (1) Men and women of full age, without any limitation due to race, nationality or religion, have the right to marry and to found a family. They are entitled to equal rights as to marriage, during marriage and at its dissolution.

(2) Marriage shall be entered into only with the free and full consent of the intending spouses.

(3) The family is the natural and fundamental group

unit of society and is entitled to protection by society and the State.

Article 17. (1) Everyone has the right to own property alone as well as in association with others.

(2) No one shall be arbitrarily deprived of his property.

Article 18. Everyone has the right to freedom of thought, conscience and religion; this right includes freedom to change his religion or belief, and freedom, either alone or in community with others and in public or private, to manifest his religion or belief in teaching practice, worship and observance.

Article 19. Everyone has the right to freedom of opinion and expression; this right includes freedom to hold opinions without interference and to seek, receive and impart information and ideas through any media and regardless of frontiers.

Article 20. (1) Everyone has the right to freedom of peaceful assembly and association.

(2) No one may be compelled to belong to an association.

Article 21. (1) Everyone has the right to take part in the government of his country, directly or through freely chosen representatives.

(2) Everyone has the right to equal access to public service in his country.

(3) The will of the people shall be the basis of the

authority of government; this will shall be expressed in periodic and genuine elections which shall be by universal and equal suffrage and shall be held by secret vote or by equivalent free voting procedure.

Article 22. Everyone, as a member of society, has the right to social security and is entitled to realization, through national effort and international co-operation and in accordance with the organization and resources of each State, of the economic, social and cultural rights indispensable for his dignity and the free development of his personality.

Article 23. (1) Everyone has the right to work, to free choice of employment, to just and favourable conditions of work and to protection against unemployment.

(2) Everyone, without any discrimination, has the right to equal pay for equal work.

(3) Everyone who works has the right to just and favourable remuneration ensuring for himself and his family an existence worthy of human dignity, and supplemented, if necessary, by other means of social protection.

(4) Everyone has the right to form and to join trade unions for the protection of his interests.

Article 24. Everyone has the right to rest and leisure, including reasonable limitation of working hours and periodic holidays with pay.

Article 25. (1) Everyone has the right to a standard of living adequate for the health and well-being of himself and of his family, including food, clothing, housing and medical care and necessary social services, and the right to security in the event of unemployment, sickness, disability, widowhood, old age or other lack of livelihood in circumstances beyond his control.
(2) Motherhood and childhood are entitled to special care and assistance. All children, whether born in or out of wedlock, shall enjoy the same social protection.
Article 26. (1) Everyone has the right to education. Education shall be free, at least in the elementary and fundamental stages. Elementary education shall be compulsory. Technical and professional education shall be made generally available and higher education shall be equally accessible to all on the basis of merit.
(2) Education shall be directed to the full development of the human personality and to the strengthening of respect for human rights and fundamental freedoms. It shall promote understanding, tolerance and friendship, among all nations, racial or religious groups, and shall further the activities of the United Nations for the maintenance of peace.
(3) Parents have a prior right to choose the kind of education that shall be given to their children.
Article 27. (1) Everyone has the right freely to participate

in the cultural life of the community, to enjoy the arts and to share; in scientific advancement and its benefits.

(2) Everyone has the right to the protection of the moral and material interests resulting from any scientific, literary or artistic production of which he is the author.

Article 28. Everyone is entitled to a social and international order in which the rights and freedoms set forth in this Declaration can be fully realized.

Article 29. (1) Everyone has duties to the community in which alone the free and full development of his personality is possible.

(2) In the exercise of his rights and freedoms, everyone shall be subject only to such limitations as are determined by law solely for the purpose of securing due recognition and respect for the rights and freedoms of others and of meeting the just requirements of morality, public order and the general welfare in a democratic society.

(3) These rights and freedoms may in no case be exercised contrary to the purposes and principles of the United Nations.

Article 30. Nothing in this Declairation may be interpreted as implying for any State, group or person any right to engage in any activity or to perform any act aimed at the destruction of any of the rights and freedoms set forth herein.

I

Introductory

Life is dynamic, and so are man and human society. One characteristic of dynamism is that it generates friction, and in terms of social values that means difference and very often dispute. Difference, or, let us say, the right to differ, lies at the root of all knowledge, inquiry investigation, research and progress. While, therefore, we must strive to safeguard the right to differ, to question, to dissent and on occasion even to protest, we must at the same time strive to secure that our differences, in every sphere-religious, philosophical, scientific, social, economic, political or whatever, should act and react beneficently and not destructively. When they threaten to become acute they must be regulated, and must be sought to be resolved or adjusted through the adoption of agreed peaceful procedures. This means, broadly, that we must all submit voluntarily or, if needed, reluctantly and even under constraint, to what has come to be described as the rule of law.

The Declaration of Human Rights does not, in the accepted juristic sense of the term, constitutes a "law". It stands, nevertheless, as a shining milestone along the long, and often difficult and weary, path trodden by Man down the corridors of History, through centuries of suffering and tribulation, towards the goal of freedom, justice and equality. Man's struggle for freedom, justice and equality has been waged in all ages and in many fields and theatres, with varying fortunes. Each of these battles, and the ground won in each, have, in turn, forwarded the cause of Man and have contributed towards the formulation and adoption of the Declaration, which is entitled to rank with the great historical documents and Charters directed towards the same objective.

Some of the written Constitutions, more particularly those of certain newly independent States, have incorporated the substance of several of the articles of the Declaration as substantive provisions, and others have set forth some of them as Directives of State policy. In the former case the relevant provisions have become justiciable and are thus enforceable through judicial process. This is encouraging, so far as it goes; but it is only a beginning. Much remains to be achieved in that regard, as well as in other respects.

At this stage the main effort must continue to be directed towards obtaining wider recognition of the need to insure that human rights shall carry with them sanctions which would serve to make these rights enforceable through judicial process. For this purpose, the principal instrument which should be availed of is the national legislature of each State, which should, through appropriate constitutional and legislative processes, invest human rights with legal sanctions enforceable through the national judicial system. This process would, however, prove effective only in the case of States in which resort to judicial process is not unduly restricted and the process is guaranteed to take its due course without let or hindrance. In other words, a free and independent judiciary is a *sine qua non* for the effective safeguarding of human rights and for guaranteeing freedom, justice and equality.

Legislative action at the national level, supported by a free and independent judiciary, would go a very long way towards securing the desired objective, but would need to be supplemented by provision of recourse, by way of appeal or review, and in suitable cases even by original motion, to regional tribunals and ultimately to an International Tribunal. Recourse to a regional or to the International Tribunal at the initial stage should, however, be available only in cases where no remedy has been provided for at the national level. Exhaustion of remedies available at the national level must be a condition precedent without fulfilment of which recourse should not be open to a regional or International Tribunal. In the absence of such a provision, the harmonious working of a system of national, regional and International Tribunals might prove both cumbersome and difficult.

Regarding legislative provisions embodying human rights, it must be remembered that the Declaration of Human Rights is not a draft Bill and cannot serve that purpose. While some of the articles of the Declaration embody clear-cut, concrete provisions and could, with slight verbal alterations, be incorporated in a draft Bill, the rest only give expression to the ideal or objective to be achieved through administrative action, possibly in stages, supported and strengthened by legislative authority. The pace and tempo in each region and country would be dependent upon many and varying factors-social, cultural, economic-and uniformity could not reasonably be insisted upon. Nor would it be wise to call for literal compliance with every article of the Declaration. Some of these, pertaining to the social and cultural fields, may, in certain systems and disciplines, be acceptable in the spirit, while calling for some modification, limitation or explanation of their scope, meaning and operation before they could be cast in the legislative mould. So long as the purpose underlying them could be carried into effect, adaptation to particular social and cultural systems and patterns would be beneficent rather than harmful.

This is the Age of Man. Man is beginning to be conscious of his own position in the universe and demands that his personality and dignity shall be accorded due recognition and respect. He is beginning to take note of that which his fellow beings, society and the State owe to him and of that which, in turn, he owes to them. This process needs to be stimulated and accelerated. This consciousness needs to be aroused where it may still be lacking and to be sharpened where it has been awakened. In this context emphasis must be laid on man's obligations and duties towards his fellow beings as the principal means of securing his own rights, freedom and privileges, for they are the obverse and reverse of the same coin. To the degree to which each of us fulfils and discharges his own duties and obligations towards his fellow beings, he promotes the climate in which human dignity, freedom and equality may flourish and achieve their consummation.

How is it that in the last half of the twentieth century, after having passed through the shattering and devastating experience of two world wars and in the shadow of a nuclear holocaust, despite all the effort that has so far been put forth to the contrary, man continues to be the victim of discrimination, intolerance and cruelty at the hands of his fellow man? One would have thought that man's daily increasing knowledge of the working of the laws of nature and his growing mastery over the forces of nature, which has opened for every one of us the prospect of a richer, fuller and happier life, would have brought in their wake an era in which man could dispense with the weapons of greed, selfishness, exploitation and dominance which had so far been regarded, albeit utterly erroneously, as contributing towards the welfare and prosperity of those who were, from time to time, in a position to employ them. For, indeed, the truth is daily becoming more manifest, as experience in every field continues to furnish fresh confirmation, that the prosperity of all is promoted through mutual sharing and co-operation rather than through the exploitation and domination of some by others. It must be our constant endeavour to bring this home to all in every corner of the globe.

While, therefore, it is not only necessary but essential that we should intensify and multiply our efforts towards the safeguarding of human rights through executive, administrative, legislative and judicial processes, we must all, individually and collectively, strive continuously to deepen our consciousness of the duties we owe to each other at the moral and spiritual levels.

For the Muslims, and indeed for all mankind, Islam seeks to stimulate and deepen that consciousness. It emphasizes our duties and obligations, so that each of us, by due discharge of them, should help to safeguard freedom, justice and equality for all and should promote and foster human welfare and prosperity in all spheres - social, economic, moral and spiritual. It seeks to establish a pattern of society which, in all the changing and developing circumstances of a dynamic world, would maintain its character of beneficence in all spheres of life - individual, domestic, national and international. For this purpose it furnishes us with a framework of beliefs, duties, obligations, exhortations and sanctions. It also provides us with guidance at all levels and in all fields.

The Prophet's functions are described in the Quran

as, the creation and strengthening of faith through drawing attention to Divine Signs, the moral and physical uplift of the people, teaching them the Law and furnishing them with guidance and expounding the philosophy underlying the Law and the guidance (62:3).

It should be noted that the Quran prescribes only those details which are essential. It thus leaves considerable room for development and safeguards against restrictive rigidity. Indeed, it warns against seeking the regulation of everything by express Divine command, as that might make the framework rigid and inelastic and, therefore, burdensome. "O ye who believe, do not keep asking about things which, if they were expounded to you, would become troublesome for you ... Allah has left them out. Allah is Most Forgiving, Forbearing. A people before you made such demands, and when they received the directions they repudiated them" (5:102-3).

That which Allah has "left out" is meant to be devised, in accord with the prescribed standards and values and in consonance with the framework, through mutual consultation (3:100:42:39) to meet the need when it should arise, always bearing in mind that the overall standard is that *ma'roof*, equity, is to be fostered and *munkar*, iniquity, is to be eschewed.

When the Prophet appointed Mu'az as Qazi of Yemen, he asked him what rule he would follow when he had to make a decision. Mu'az said he would look for the rule in the Book of Allah. "And if you do not find the answer in the Book?" queried the Prophet. "I shall seek for it in the example of the Prophet." "And if you still lack an answer?" "I shall exercise my own judgment." "That is the right way," he was assured by the Prophet.[1]

The whole vast, elaborate system of Muslim jurisprudence has been developed along those lines. In fact Islam stimulated and released so effervescent and variegated an intellectual ferment that, to confine oneself to the field of jurisprudence alone, within a very brief period several Schools of Jurisprudence flourished within the rapidly widening expanse of the Islamic State. Four of them, the Hanafi, Maliki, Shafei and Hanbali (all of the Sunni persuasion) still maintain their preeminence and hold their sway in regions where Islamic Law is administered.

The great Imams of Jurisprudence, Sunni and Shia alike, and also those of other persuasions, together with their eminent disciples and a host of those who

[1] Tirmidhi I, Sect.: Judgments, Ch.: Problems facing a Judge, etc.

followed after them have, through their unremitting labours sustained through centuries, not only enriched and embellished Muslim Jurisprudence, but made an invaluable contribution to the development of the Science of Law and to what that eminent international jurist C. Wilfred Jenks, has called the Common Law of Mankind. They have thus laid the juristic world under a heavy debt of gratitude.

But if one might, without impertinence, venture so to describe a portion of their intellectual exercises, they built not only truly but more vastly than was needed. In their studies they did not content themselves with considering the concrete and practical situations that needed to be resolved, but travelled on to the theoretical and hypothetical, which might never be encountered. They conceived, no doubt, that they were in this manner widening the horizon of jurisprudence, but as it proved, they succeeded only in restricting it. Their speculations concerning hypothetical problems and situations served to freeze the further development of jurisprudence, which over a long period thereafter became more speculative than constructive.

Those of lesser stature who followed them, finding that little of the practical or even of the hypothetical was left for the exercise of their scholarship, talent and intellect, began on occasion to tread amusing and curious byways. So much so that some of the so-called works on Jurisprudence of later periods comprise within their scope sections entitled *Bab-el-Hiyal*, i.e. Chapters on Evasion, which work out methods of evading the spirit and defeating the purpose of the law while complying with its letter! It is obvious that the result was mortifying rather than enlivening, and the development of Muslim Jurisprudence was not only arrested but suffered a severe set-back.

For close upon a century now, Muslim thought, in all its aspects, has experienced a healthy revival, the effects of which are today open to observation and appraisal in every field. This has, however, not always been welcome among certain sections of Western scholars of Islam. For them the medieval exercises in speculation hold a fascination from which they find it hard to release themselves. The concrete and practical are too cold for their liking and lack the flavour of romance to which they have accustomed themselves. Yet if they would only take the trouble to face about, they would meet in the greater part of today's Muslim thought-exegesis, ethics, jurisprudence spiritual values, etc.-a refreshing, purifying and uplifting quality which they would be glad to welcome. Many of their colleagues have already discovered this, and without abandoning any part of what indeed is of truth and tremendous value in the rich legacy and abundant inheritance- of Islam, they have turned eagerly to what Islam has to offer in the age which is now opening out before us.

In studying the Universal Declaration of Human Rights from the Islamic point of view, we must remember that while Islam lays down broad values and standards which clearly endorse the spirit and purpose of the Declaration, it does not pronounce verbatim on all the specific provisions of the Declaration.

Some of the Articles of the Declaration restate and emphasize fundamental rights and principles, while others only declare and draw attention to objectives and ideals which should be progressively pursued as the aims of State policy. Still others spell out methods of giving effect to what is considered imperative or eminently desirable in today's conditions as a practical expression of the enjoyment of freedom, justice and equality. The Declaration does not purport to be exhaustive, as, in the nature of things, no formulation of human rights could claim finality. Equally, it cannot be claimed that its provisions may not call for amendment or modification as the result of experience gained or of changes that may be introduced into the social, economic or political patterns of society and the State. For instance, the first half of the first sentence of Article 12 and the second paragraph of Article 13 would not have suggested themselves so readily to a Commission on Human Rights submitting a draft declaration in the early years of the present century. On the other hand, when the political unity of Western Europe begins to assume practical shape, some re-wording of Article 15 might be indicated, while the development of World Federation, or some form of World Government or World Community, might entail a reappraisal of the whole concept of nationality, which is none too precise as it is.

Again, it is presumed that acceptance or endorsement of the Declaration would not oblige a society or State to give literal effect to the provisions of every article. This may not be practicable in some cases, or might tend to defeat the very purpose in view. So far as States are concerned, that aspect could be taken care of in the Protocol embodying the declaration of adherence of a State to the Covenant of Human Rights. So far as particular societies may be involved, it would be desirable to obviate any conflict of values by directing effort towards securing, promoting and strengthening the spirit of the Declaration and its overall objectives rather than insisting upon literal compliance with each specific detail. A certain degree of diversity and flexibility in the cultural field should be welcomed and safeguarded, so long as it does not offend against the ideal purpose, rather than looked upon as something which needs to be ironed out.

II

Man and the Universe

Islam is an Arabic word, derived from a root which means both "peace" and "submission". It thus connotes the attainment of peace, here and Hereafter, through submission to Allah, or, in other words, through conformity to His Will. A person who thus submits is a Muslim. In the Quran (the scripture of Islam), the appellation "Muslim" is applied to all the righteous.

For intance, Abraham is described as "ever inclined to God and in submission to Him [Muslim]" (2:68). "When his Lord said to him: Do thou submit, he responded: I have submitted to the Lord of the worlds. The same did Abraham enjoin upon his sons-and so did Jacob, saying: O my sons, truly Allah has chosen this religion for you; so let not death overtake you except when you are in a state of submission [Muslim]" (2:132-133).

When death came to Jacob. "he said to his sons: What will you worship after me? They answered: We shall worship thy God, the God of thy fathers, Abraham, Ishmael and Isaac, the One God; and to Him we submit ourselves [Muslims]" (2:J 14).

Joseph is mensioned as praying: "O my Lord. Thou hast bestowed power upon me and taught me the interpretation of dreams. O Maker of the heavens and the earth. Thou art my Protector in this world and the Hereafter. Let death come to me in a state of submission to Thy will [Muslim] and join me to the righteous" (12:102).

Concerning the disciples of Jesus it is stated: "I inspired the disciples (of Jesus) to believe in Me and My Messenger (Jesus). They said: We believe and bear Thou witness that we have submitted [are Muslims]" (5:112).

Jesus "said: Who will be my helpers in the cause of Allah? The disciples answered: We are helpers in the cause of Allah. We have believed in Allah, and bear thou witness that we are obedient [Muslims]" (3:53).

So with every Prophet; those who accepted a Prophet and submitted to the Divine Will as revealed through him were Muslims. As, however, the term was given currency by the Quran, its application has become limited to those who profess belief in Islam.

Islam represents the culmination of the evolutionary process in revelation. "This day have I perfected your religion for you and completed My favour unto you and have chosen for you Islam as religion" (5:4).

The Quran, however, affirms the truth of all previous revelations and the righteousness of all previous Prophets.

It starts with the position that no people has been left without revealed guidance. This flows from God's attribute of Providence. He is not only the Creator of the Universe but also sustains, nourishes and leads it stage by stage towards perfection. It is with that connotation that He is designated "Lord of all the worlds" (1:2). There is also the clear affirmation, "Verily, We have sent there with the truth, as a bearer of glad tidings and as a Warner, and there is no people to whom a Warner has not been sent" (35:25).

A Muslim is required to believe in the truth of previous revelations and in the righteousness of all Prophets.

"Say ye: We believe in Allah and in that which has been revealed to us, and in that which was revealed to Abraham and Ishmael, and Isaac, and Jacob and his children, and in what was given to Moses and Jesus and what was given to all other Prophets from their Lord.

We make no difference between any of them, and to Him we submit ourselves;" (2:137).

"We gave him (Abraham) Isaac and Jacob; each did We guide aright, and Noah did We guide aright aforetime, and of his progeny. David and Solomon and Job and Joseph and Moses and Aaron. Thus do We reward those who do good.

"And We guided Zachariah and John and Jesus and Elias: each one of them was of the righteous.

"We also guided Ishmael and Isaiah and Jonah and Lot; and each one did We exalt above the people.

"We also exalted some of their fathers and their children and their brethren, and We chose them and guided them in the straight path.

"That is the guidance of Allah. He guides thereby those of His servants whom He pleases. If they had worshipped aught beside Him, surely all they did would have been of no avail to them.

"It is these to whom We gave the Book and dominion and prophethood ... These it is whom Allah guided aright, so follow thou their guidance" (6:85-91).

This does not mean that the Quran makes obligatory upon the Muslims all the commandments and ordinances contained in today's version of the previous revelations and Scriptures. Indeed, it emphasizes repeatedly that these versions have suffered grievously at the hands of some of those who profess to be their supporters (2:80). What the Quran affirms is the actual revelation vouchsafed to the previous Prophets. Thus: "Surely, We sent down the Torah wherein is guidance and light. By it did the Prophets, who were obedient to Us, judge for the Jews, as did the godly people and those learned in the Law" (5:45). And again: "And We caused Jesus, son of Mary, to follow in their footsteps, fulfilling that which was revealed before him in the Torah; and We gave him the Gospel which contained guidance and light, fulfilling that which was revealed before that in the Torah as an admonition for the God-fearing" (5:47). The Gospel here means the revelation vouchsafed to Jesus, and not the books which are today commonly so described.

Not only are today's versions of previous revelations open to serious question on the score of authenticity of the text and accuracy of translation and interpretation, many of the details concerning commandments and ordinances and even doctrine, which were of a temporary or local character, are now out of date or inapplicable. Today's doctrine is also in many cases based on subsequent interpretation and formulation which appear to have little connection with what was contained in the revelation and even contradict it. Attention is drawn to all this in the Quran, and yet the Quran emphasizes the unity of the fundamental teaching contained in all previous Scriptures and insisted upon by the Prophets, namely belief in the Existence and Unity of God and in the Hereafter, and conformity to God's will through righteous action.

Previous revelations were limited in their scope. Each was designed to meet the needs of the people to whom it was sent during the stage of development upon which that people was about to enter. Each contained fundamental truths, valid through the ages in respect of the whole of mankind, but it also contained guidance, directions, commandments and prohibitions which were of a local or temporary character. Moreover, in course of time, portions of those revelations were lost or forgotten. That which was of universal and permanent application in previous revelations is reaffirmed in the Quran. Such portions as had been lost or were overlooked or forgotten, but were still needed, are revived. That which was of purely local or temporary application and was no longer needed, is omitted. That which was not contained in previous revelations, the need for it not yet having arisen, but which would henceforth be needed by mankind, is added (2:107; 3:8).

Thus the Quran, while affirming the truth of all previous revelations, itself comprises all truth for the whole of mankind for all time. It is described as "pure Scriptures, comprising lasting commandments" (98:3-4).

The Quran is thus a universal possession and inheritance, its message is directed to the whole of mankind (7:159). It is sent down as guidance for mankind, with clear proofs of guidance and with discrimination between truth and falsehood (2:186).

It expounds and explains all that is or may be needed by mankind for the complete fulfilment of life (16:90). It seeks to create faith in God through rehearsal of God's Signs: it makes provision for mankind's welfare, material, moral and spiritual; it teaches all that is needed for beneficent regulation of human life and expounds the philosophy underlying it, so that reason being satisfied, wholehearted conformity to what is taught may be assured (62:2-3). It expounds the significance of establishing and maintaining communion with God. It draws attention to various Divine attributes, their operation and the manner in which mankind may derive benefit from the knowledge thereof. In short, all that is basic for the promotion of human welfare in all spheres, whether pertaining to principles or conduct, is set forth and expounded (16:90).

It is this comprehensiveness of the Quran, the need to make provision for guidance in every respect for all peoples for all time, that made it necessary that the guidance should be conveyed in verbal revelation. The Quran is literally the Word of God, and possesses the quality of being alive, as the universe is alive. It is not possible to set forth at any time the whole meaning and interpretation of the Quran or, indeed, of any portion of it with finality. It yields new truths and fresh guidance in every age and at every level. It is a standing and perpetual miracle (18:110).

The world is dynamic and so is the Quran. Indeed, so dynamic is the Quran that it has always been found to keep ahead of the world and never to lag behind it. However fast the pace at which the pattern of human life may change, the Quran always yields, and will go on yielding, the needed guidance in advance. This has now been demonstrated through more than thirteen centuries, and that is a guarantee that it will continue to be demonstrated through the ages.

The Quran has proclaimed that falsehood will never overtake it. All research into the past and every discovery and invention of the future will affirm its truth (41:43). The Quran speaks at every level; it seeks to reach every type of understanding, through parables, similitudes, arguments, reasoning, the observation and study of the phenomena of nature, and the natural, moral and spiritual laws (18:55; 39:28; 59:22).

It reasons from the physical and tangible to the spiritual and intangible. For instance: "Among His Signs is this; that thou seest the earth lying withered, but when We send down water on it, it stirs and quickens with verdure. Surely He Who quickens the earth can quicken the dead. Verily, He has power over all things" (41:40). Here by quickening of the dead is meant the revival and rebirth of a people. As the dead earth is quickened by life-giving rain from heaven, a people that appears to be dead in all respects is revived and regenerated through spiritual water from the heavens, that is to say, through Divine revelation. This idea is expressed in the Quran in several places. Both resurrection and renaissance are explained with reference to the phenomenon of the dead earth being revived through life-giving rain (22:6-8).

The Quran repeatedly urges observation and reflection, the exercise of reason, and understanding (22:270). For instance: "In the creation of the heavens and the earth and in the alternation of the night and the day there are indeed Signs for men of understanding, who remember Allah while standing, sitting, and lying down, and ponder the creation of the heavens and the earth. This leads them to exclaim: Our Lord, Thou hast not created all this without purpose; Holy art Thou" (3:191-192).

Whenever attention is drawn in the Quran to God's Signs, the object is to urge reflection upon the event or phenomenon cited, that we may proceed to draw lessons therefrom which will help us to grasp the Truth; to understand the operation of Divine attributes and of Divine laws; to appreciate spiritual values and to adjust and order our lives accordingly, so that all our activities in every sphere may become wholly beneficent. It is in that sense that the guidance contained in the Quran is described as "a healing and a mercy for those who put their faith in it" (17:83). We are reminded: "O mankind, there has indeed come to you an exhortation from your Lord and a healing for whatever ills there are in the hearts, and a guidance and a mercy for those who believe" (10:58).

With all this, man is left to his own free choice in acceptance of the Truth. Faith is not commanded on the basis of authority, but is invited on the basis of understanding (12:109). "This is a Book that We have revealed to thee, full of blessings, that they may reflect over its verses, and that those gifted with understanding may take heed" (38:30). There is complete freedom to believe or to reject. "Say to them: It is the Truth from your Lord; therefore let him who will, believe, and let him who will, disbelieve" (18:30). But of course, though the choice is free, the consequences of the choice follow in accordance with Divine law. No one is forced. Everyone must choose and seek the purpose of his life on the basis of faith or turn his back upon the Truth and destroy his soul, according to his choice.

The Quran has been described as a Light and as a clear Book, whereby "does Allah guide those who seek His pleasure along the paths of peace, and lead them out of every kind of darkness into the light by His will, and guide them along the right path" .(5:16-17).

On the other hand, the Quran itself discourages the tendency to seek regulation of everything by Divine command, pointing out that such regulation would become restrictive and burdensome (5:102).

The Quran contains Divine assurance that the guidance embodied therein will be guarded under Divine protection (15:10). This comprises several aspects:

First, the text of the revelation should be preserved in its purity and entirety for all time. Considering that the revelation contained in the Quran was vouchsafed to the Prophet over a period of twenty-two years, first in Mecca and then in Medina, that this period was marked by persecution, disturbance and fighting, that the Prophet himself was not literate, and that there was no sure method of preserving a record of the revelation except through human memory, it is a truly miraculous fact that the text of the Quran has been preserved absolutely pure and entire, down to the last vowel point. Even non-Muslim scholars, who do not accept the Quran as Divine revelation, affirm that the Quran is word for word that which Muhammad gave out to the world as Divine revelation.

Second, the language in which the revelation was sent should continue in use as a living language. Classical Arabic is today understood and used as a means of communication over much vaster areas of the earth and by many hundred times more people than was the case in the time of the Prophet.

These factors, so essential for the safeguarding of the guidance contained in the revelation, could not have been assured by the Prophet in advance. Yet they are not enough. For life is dynamic, and the pattern of human life is subject to constant change. The process of evolution is at work all the time. Besides, history testifies that the passage of time brings about a decline in spiritual and moral values in a civilisation. It is inevitable, therefore, that over the centuries there should occur a falling-off in the true appreciation of Divine guidance set forth in Divine revelation as applicable to current conditions and situations. The complete safeguarding of Divine revelation thus necessitates a constant process of spiritual revival and rebirth. In the nature of things this must also come about through revelation. It was announced by the Prophet that to meet this need God would continue to raise from among the Muslims, at the beginning of each century, someone who would be inspired to revive the faith by drawing attention to the guidance contained in the Quran apposite to existing conditions.[2] History has confirmed the truth of this assurance conveyed by the Prophet.

The last half-century has, however, witnessd the onset of a tremendous revolution in human values in all spheres of life. Standards that had been accepted and subscribed to through centuries are undergoing rapid revision and modification. The very dimensions of human life are being reshaped, so that scholars and thinkers are beginning to stress the need of a new

[2] Abu Daud II, Sect.: Al-malahim.

revelation. Yet the Quran is quite clear that the guidance contained therein will be found adequate during all stages at all times.

What provision, it may be asked, is there in the Quran to meet the contingency with which mankind is faced today, and which is likely to grow ever more insistent during all the tomorrows that lie ahead? To meet this contingency the Quran announced that the Prophet not only had been raised up in the generation among whom he lived, but would also be raised up among others "who have not yet joined them" (62:3-4). This means a spiritual second advent of the Prophet for the purpose of setting forth from the Quran guidance that may be needed in the New Age, and for illustrating the values demanded by the exigencies with which man may be faced. This promise has been fulfilled in the advent of Ahmad, of Qadian (1835-1908), who warned that mankind stood at the threshold of an era which would bear the same relationship to his age-that is, the beginning of the twentieth century-as the beginning of that century bore to the days of Adam, and who proceeded to set forth from the Quran, in the light of revelation vouchsafed to him, the guidance that mankind now desperately needs.

The most striking characteristic of Islam is its universality and the place that it assigns to man as the centre of the universe. Islam teaches and insists upon the acceptance and comprehension of the Unity of the Creator, which results in the unity and co-ordination of creation and the unity and equality of man.

Once this fundamental is accepted and grasped the rest becomes easily comprehensible and the necessary co-ordination and adjustment will follow as a matter of course. Indeed these must become compulsive if confusion, chaos and destruction are to be avoided and peace, prosperity and human welfare in all spheres of life are to be promoted and strengthened.

The object of Islam is to establish a balance and to bring about accord in the relationship of man to his Maker, to the Universe and to his fellow men through beneficent adjustment ((55:8-10).

The primary object of all revelation is to emphasize the concept of God and to explain the relationship between God and the Universe and the place of man in that juxtaposition.

The Quran is clear and emphatic on the Unity of God and utterly condemns any doctrine, idea or concept which might directly or indirectly tend to associate any other thing or being with God as a partner or equal. Proclaim: "He is Allah, the One, Allah, the Independent and Besought of All. He begets not, nor is He begotten! There is none like unto Him" (112:2-5).

This concept is reinforced by various arguments. For instance: "Allah has not taken unto Himself any son, nor is there any other god along with Him; in that case, each god would have taken away what he had created, and some of them would surely have dominated over others. Glorify, then, Allah above all that which they attribute to Him. Knower of the unseen and of the seen; exalted is He, there fore, above all that which they associate with Him" (23:92-93). Mythology furnishes ample illustration of the confusion and chaos that would prevail if there were a plurality of gods. There would be an end to all certainty and order and consequently to all beneficence. Man and the universe, instead of being manifestations of Divine beneficence, would present a spectacle of capricious and cruel sport, and instead of progressing constantly towards perfection, would be speedily destroyed. "If there had been in the heavens and the earth other gods besides Allah, then surely the twain would have come to ruin. Glorified then be Allah, the Lord of Power, above what they attribute" (21:23).

It follows that all adoration, glorification, worship and obedience are due to God alone. He is the object of the heart's deepest love and devotion. To seek nearness to Him, to do His will in all things, to win His pleasure, in short to become the manifestation of His attributes, that is to say, His image, is the purpose of man's creation (51-57). He is the Source of all beneficence, everything proceeds from Him and is dependent upon Him, He is Independent and stands in no need of help or assistance from any other source. All sources and means proceed from Him, and nothing exists or subsists outside His control or authority. "Allah bears witness that there is no god but He, and so do the angels and those possessed of knowledge; Maintainer of Justice, there is no god but He, the Mighty, the Wise" (3:19).

The Quran teaches that God has throughout affirmed and borne witness to His Existence, His Unity and His various attributes, and revealed these to mankind for the complete fulfilment of life in all spheres.

The discovery of all this was not left to man. In other words, the Quran repudiates the notion that man, through the use of his intellect, progressively perfected his own concept of the Divine.

Had that been so, countless generations would have perished in ignorance before a concept of God even remotely approaching the reality could have been evolved.

Thus the Quran does not countenance the thesis that man's concept of God has evolved progressively from the worship of natural objects to the recognition and acceptance of a Universal Almighty Creator. This would have meant that man created God through a process of intellectual exercise. God has ever revealed Himself. "He sends down the angels with revelation by His command on whomsoever of His servants He pleases, directing: Warn that there is no god but I, so take Me alone for your Protector" (16:3).

God is not merely the First Cause. He is the Creator, the Maker, the Fashioner, and He exercises control over the universe at all times. "Allah is the Creator of all things, and He is the Guardian over all things. To Him belong the keys of the heavens and the earth" (39:63-64). All His attributes are eternal. None of them ever falls into disuse. His attribute of Creation is equally in operation all the time. "Allah originates Creation; then He repeats it; then to Him shall you be brought back" (30:12). "To Him belongs whatsoever is in the heavens and the earth. All are obedient to Him. He it is Who originates the Creation, then repeats it, for it is most easy for Him. His is the most exalted state in the heavens and the earth. He is the Mighty, the Wise" (30:27-28).

He creates and perfects; He designs and guides (87:3-4). He has bestowed upon everything its appropriate form, which would enable each thing to perform its functions properly, and has then guided everything to its proper function (21:51). He bestows life and He causes death (53:45), and to Him do all things ultimately return (53:43).

"To Allah belongs the kingdom of the heavens and the earth, and He has mastery over everything" (3:190). Having created the universe and all that is in it, He did not sit back and, as it were, abdicate His control over it. Nothing can continue in existence except with His constant support. "In His hand is the dominion over all things and He grants protection to everything, but against Him there is no protection" (23:89).

Nature and all its phenomena, life and all its exigencies, including its termination here below, have all been created in God's wisdom, obey His laws, and are under His control (21:34; 36:38-41; 67:2-5).

God regulates it all and clearly explains His Signs that men may have firm belief in communion with Him and in their accountability to Him (13:3).

The attributes of God have been set out in the Quran in different contexts. He forgives faults and shortcomings, He accepts repentance, He judges and imposes penalties, He is the Lord of Bounty. Towards Him is the final return (40:4).

It follows that, according to the Quran, the Universe did not just happen or grow of itself. It was created, and was created with a purpose. The Quran teaches that it would be inconsistent with the very concept of the Divine that He should bring something into being merely by way of sport or pastime. “We created not the heaven and the earth and all that is between the two in sport. If We had wished to find a pastime We would surely have found it in what is with Us, if at all We were to do such a thing” (21:17-18). Indeed, to imagine that God would do anything without purpose would amount in effect to a denial of God. ”We have not created the heaven and the earth and all that is between them in vain. That is the view of those who deny Us” (38:28).

All God’s attributes operate in accordance with the requirements of wisdom (71:14). The creation of the heavens and the earth was also in accord with the requirements of wisdom (15:86; 39:6). The whole of God’s creation is in harmony. There is no discord, disorder or incongruity.

Everything is adjusted and co-ordinated so as to carry out the purpose for which it was created (67:2-5).

Such disorder or maladjustment as may be observed, or may occur, results from misuse or contravention of the laws governing the universe.

The purpose of the creation of the universe is to aid man in achieving the object for which he was created. This is part of God's unlimited bounty to man. The universe and the laws that govern it constantly work out, under Divine direction, the consequences beneficent or otherwise, of man's use of God's bounties (14:8; 16:11-19; 56:69-75).

The creation of man has passed through many stages (71:15-18). Having been originated from water and clay, over millennia, man began to be created from the sperm, was endowed with sense and understanding, and having thus been perfected, began to be guided through revelation (23:13-15; 32:7-10; 35:12).

The Quran stresses the unity of mankind, that man has been created of one kind (4:2; 16:73). Like the universe, man has not been created without purpose, to live aimlessly (57:37). His life has a purpose and he is responsible and accountable in respect of it. In the Quran, the principle of accountability is expressed in terms of man having to be "brought back" to God (23:16). The purpose of man's creation is that he should receive the impress of God's attributes and should, within the limits of his capacities, become a manifestation of them. In other words men, high and low, have been created so that they should become God's image (51:57). To aid man in the achievement of this purpose he has been endowed with appropriate faculties and capacities. "Surely We have created man in the best mould" (95:5). In addition, God has constrained the whole of the universe to the service of man, which means that the universe is governed by laws and that the operation of these laws has as its object the beneficent service of man. These laws are ascertainable and through their knowledge man can progressively increase his mastery over the forces of nature and extract greater and greater beneficence from them.

The Quran describes man as God's "vicegerent upon earth" (2:31). It affirms that man having been created by stages and his faculties having been perfected, he began to be guided through revelation. He then found that the universe was subjected to him for the enrichment and fulfilment of his life.

"Allah it is Who has subjected the sea to you that ships may sail thereon by His command, and that you may seek of His Bounty and that you may draw benefit therefrom. He has subjected to you whatsoever is in the heavens and whatsoever is in the earth; all of it. In that surely are Signs for a people who reflect" (45:13-14).

Again:

"Allah is He Who created the heavens and the earth

and caused water to come down from the clouds and brought forth therewith fruit for your sustenance; and He has subjected to you the ships that they may sail through the sea by His command, and the rivers too has He subjected to you. He has also subjected to you the sun and the moon, both pursuing their courses constantly. He has subjected to you the night as well as the day. He gave you all that you wanted of Him. If you try to count the favours of Allah, you will not be able to number them. Verily, man is apt to misuse and abuse the bounties of Allah" (14:33-35).

God's favour in bestowing upon man all that was needed for the fulfilment of the purpose of life and in subjecting to his service the whole of the universe and all its phenomena is repeatedly stressed, and man is exhorted to reflect upon, and to draw lessons from, all these phenomena. "He it is Who sends down water for you from the clouds; from it you have your drink; and there grows by it vegetation on which you pasture your beasts.

"Therewith He also grows for you corn and the olive. and the date palm, and the grape, and all kinds of fruit. Surely in that is a Sign for a people who reflect.

"He has constrained into service the things He has created for you in the earth, of diverse hues. Surely, in that is a Sign for a people who take heed.

"He it is Who has subjected to you the sea, that you may take therefrom flesh to eat, and the ornaments that you wear. And thou seest the ships ploughing it, that you may journey thereby, and that you may seek of His bounty, and that you may be grateful" (16:11-15).

References to God's Signs emphasize the need for study and research so that the proper use of each thing may be discovered by acquiring knowledge of its properties and the laws governing them.

These gifts and bounties are for the benefit of mankind as such; that is to say, of the whole of mankind without discrimination. They are not intended for, or confined to, any particular section.

Thus, equipped with his own inherent faculties and capacities appropriate to, and adequate for, the purpose of achieving his object in life; with Divine guidance available at all stages, adequate to his needs; and with the whole of the universe subjected to his service, man has, through Divine beneficence, been placed in the most favourable position for the complete fulfilment of his lif e and for the achievement of its goal and purpose.

We can now appreciate the position allotted to man in the Divine scheme of the universe, according to the Quran. Man in this context signifies mankind, all men without distinction or discrimination. The message of Islam is directed towards and comprehends the whole of mankind. "Say: O mankind, truly I am a Messenger to you all from Allah to Whom belongs the kingdom of the heavens and the earth. There is no god but He. He gives life and He causes death" (7:159).

The Quran teaches that man's nature is pure, "the nature made by Allah; the nature in which He has created mankind" (30:31) and that evil enters from outside. The Prophet said: "Every child is born in accord with divine nature, it is his parents who make him a Jew a Zoroastrian or a Christian".[3] In other words a child is influenced by heredity and environment. It has no natural propensity towards evil.

Should man fall into evil by error or design, he can win back to purity and righteousness through prayer and repentance. "O My servants who have committed excesses against your own souls, despair not of the mercy of Allah; surely Allah forgives all sins, verily He is Most Forgiving, Merciful. Turn ye to your Lord and submit yourselves to Him before there comes unto you the chastisement" (39:54-55). And again: "Whoso believes in Allah and acts righteously, He will remove

---

[3] Bukhari I, Section: Funerals; Ch.:Children of non-Muslims.

from them the evil consequences of their deeds" (64:10).

The double assurance that everything in the universe is governed by law, the knowledge of which can be pro gressively acquired by man, and that the universe is subjected to man's service and thus is wholly beneficent, throws wide open to man all avenues of knowledge, which he is not only encouraged, but is repeatedly urged and exhorted, to explore unceasingly. The only limitation is imposed by God's law that so long as man continues to make beneficent use of God's bounties, He will continue to multiply them unto him without limit but that, on the other hand, if he misuses them, or abuses them he will be called to account in respect of them and these very bounties may become the instruments of his destruction (14:8). To this is added the assurance that Divine guidance will always be available to assist mankind in regulating human life along beneficent lines in all spheres.

III

Social Values

All values affecting man are based upon the concept that every human being is capable of achieving the highest stage of moral and spiritual development and that his personality must be respected. The Quran takes note of diversities of race, colour, language, wealth, etc., which serve their own useful purpose in the social scheme, and describes them as Signs of God for those who hear and possess knowledge (30:23). But none of these confers any privilege or imposes any disability. The Quran says that God has divided mankind into tribes and nations for greater facility of intercourse. Neither membership of a tribe nor citizen ship of a State confers any privilege, nor are they sources of honour. The true source of honour in the sight of God is a righteous life (49:14). In his Farewell Address, the Prophet said: "You are all brothers and are all equal. None of you can claim any privilege or any superiority over any other. An Arab is not to be preferred to a non-Arab, nor is a non-Arab to be preferred to an Arab; nor is a white man to be preferred to a coloured one, or a coloured one to a white, except on the basis of righteousness" .[4]

Islam has established a universal brotherhood. It is stressed that true brotherhood can be established only by virture of our relationship with one another through God. Other factors-common interests, common pursuits, common occupations-may help to foster friendship and brotherhood to a degree, but the very same factors may also engender jealousy and hostility. It is only the consciousness that mankind are all equally creatures and servants of God and that they must all constantly seek the pleasure of God, that can bring about the realization of true brotherhood, which can stand the test of all the contingencies to which life is subject. "Hold fast, all together, by the rope of Allah, and be not divided; and remember the favour of Allah, which He bestowed upon you when you were enemies and He united your hearts in love, so that by His grace you became as brethren; and you were on the brink of a pit of fire, and He saved you from it. Thus does Allah

---

[4] Hanbal V, p. 411.

explain to you His commandments, that you may be rightly guided" (3:104).

The family is the basic unit of human society. The foundation of a family is laid through marriage. One of the principal considerations to be kept in mind in the choice of a spouse is set out in one of the three or four verses that the Prophet always recited on the occasion of the celebration of a marriage. "O ye who believe, fear Allah and let every soul look to what it sends forth for the morrow" (59:19). This means that the choice should be determined not only with reference to obvious and immediate considerations, but also with reference to the more lasting consequences of the contemplated union, both in this life and in the next. The Prophet said: "Some people marry for the sake of beauty, others for family connections, others for wealth, but your choice should be determined by moral and spiritual considerations, as these are the sources of lasting happiness".[5] Degrees of kinship within which marriage is prohibited are laid down (4:23-25).

It is one of the bounties of God that He has created male and female of the same species and has put love and tenderness between them, so that they constitute a

---

[5] Muslim I, Sect.:Giving Suck to Children.

source of peace and rest for each other. "In that surely are Signs for a people who reflect" (30:32). The relationship between husband and wife is described as that of a garment to its wearer. The Quran says that a wife is raiment for the husband, and the husband is raiment for the wife (2:188). A garment provides protection, comfort and ornament. It is also the closest thing to a person outside his or her own self. A husband and wife bound together by the "love and tenderness" that God has put between them are surely garments for each other. The Quran says that the best garment is the garment of righteousness (7:2), so that a husband and wife should be such a garment for each other.

Women have rights vis-u-vis men corresponding to those that men have vis-u-vis women on a basis of fairness and equity (2:229). Men are exhorted to consort with their wives in kindness and are reminded: "If you dislike them, it may be that you dislike something wherein Allah has placed much good" (4:20).

The Prophet said: "The best among you is he who treats the members of his family best".[6] He was himself always most careful and considerate in respect of all that concerned women. On one occasion he was on

[6] Ibn Majah, Sect.:Marriage, Ch.:Good behaviour towards women.

a journey when women were also of the party. At one stage the camel drivers, fearing they were late, began to drive the camels fast. The Prophet admonished them: "Mind the crystal", meaning that they should have due regard to the comfort of the women.[7] His reference to the women as "crystal" implied that woman is delicate and sensitive, and is easily hurt. On another occasion, he explained that woman is by nature like a rib,[8] meaning that a woman performs her function in the scheme of things adequately by virtue of the very qualities in which she differs from man and that it would be foolish on the part of man to attempt to cast her into his own mould. Her charm lies in being what she is and not in being just a double or copy of man.

Islam does not regard marriage as an indissoluble sacrament. It is a civil contract, imposing mutual duties and obligations. An essential feature of the contract is a settlement by the husband on the wife, called dower (4:5), so that the wife whall own some property of her own over which she may have complete control. Divorce is permitted in Islam, but the Prophet said that of all things permitted, the most obnoxious in the sight of

7 Bukhari IV, Sect.:Good Behaviour.

8 Bukhari III, Sect.:Marriage; Ch.:Benevolence towards women.

God is divorce.[9] The process of divorce is spread over a period, during which every effort must be made to smooth out differences and bring about reconciliation. If differences become acute, the counsel and help of mediators, one from the wife's people and one from the husband's, should be sought (4:36). If divorce is finally decided upon, the husband cannot take away from the wife anything he has given her (4:21-22), and must make suitable provision for her over a period of months, which is normally required for the process to be completed. If husband and wife are reconciled to each other during this period, the divorce proceedings are cancelled (2:229-230).

Islam permits a plurality of wives, not exceeding four, but only on condition of strict equality of treatment among them. "If you fear you will not be able to deal justly with them, then marry only one" (4:4). The permission may be availed of in a national or domestic emergency, or where circumstances make it desirable that the ordinary rule of monogamy be departed from; but in every case, whatever the degree of affection that the husband may have for one wife as compared with the other, his treatment of each must

9 Abu Daud II, Sect.:Divorce; Ch.:Divorce is obnoxious.

be absolutely equal. He must make identical provision for each and spend the same period of time with each. There are detailed regulations and instructions which show that he who avails himself of the permission must submit himself to a severe discipline. The contingency that necessitates recourse to a plurality of wives may be worth the discipline, but there is certainly no scope for self-indulgence. The Prophet has said: "A man who marries two women and then does not deal justly with them will be resurrected with half his faculties paralyzed".[10] Preservation of the higher values and promotion of righteousness must be the constant objectives. Permission to marry more than one woman at a time is a necessary emergency provision for the preservation and fostering of high social values and for safeguarding society against promiscuity. In the Islamic social system no stigma attaches to the institution. Each wife occupies an equal position of dignity and honour and there is no discrimination among the children. The permission has undoubtedly been abused, but Islamic society is seeking to eradicate such abuse through legal regulation of the institution.

Great stress is laid on the proper upbringing and

---

10 Tirmidhi I, Sect.:Marniage, Ch.:Equality of Treatment.

training of children. Attention must be paid to the child's proper training long before its birth. The prayer taught by the Prophet, "O Lord, safeguard us against evil and safeguard the issue that Thou mightst bestow upon us against evil",[11] when husband and wife come together, is a striking reminder of the duty that parents owe to their children in this respect. The prayers taught in the Quran in this context have the same object. Abraham's prayer. "Lord, bestow upon me righteous offspring" (37:101), and Zachariah's prayer, "Lord, bestow upon me from Thyself pure offspring" (3:39), illustrate this. So also the prayers, "Our Lord, grant us of our wives and children the delight of our eyes, and make us a model for the righteous (25:75) and "Lord. make my offspring righteous" (46:16). The Prophet said, "Honour your children and make provision for their proper upbringing",[12] which draws attention to their being brought up in ways of righteousness so as to make them worthy of honour. One aspect of the commandment of the Quran, "Do not destroy your offspring" (17:32), is that the development of their

11 Bukhari II, Sect.:Ablutions, Ch.:Calling on Allah.

12 Ibn Maja II, Sect.:Upbringing, Ch.:Beneficence of Parents and Benevolence towards Daughters.

faculties and capacities should not be neglected, as that would amount to destroying them.

Infanticide, which was a common practice during certain periods of human history, is prohibited (17:32). The practice, prevailing in certain Arab families who prided themselves on their noble status, of infanticide of female children, is severely condemned (81:9-10). As women and female children were generally held in low esteem among the Arabs, the Prophet was very emphatic on proper upbringing of girls, and on due consideration being shown to women. He said: "A person who is blessed with a daughter or daughters and makes no discrimination between them and his sons and brings them up with kindness and affection, will be as close to me in Paradise as my forefinger and middle finger are to each other".[13]

While stressing kindness and affection towards children and uniformly treating all children tenderly, he did not approve of undue indulgence. He had laid it down as a rule for himself and his family and all his descendants that they should not accept charity. On one occasion when a quantity of dates was brought to the

[13] Muslim II, Sect.:Beneficence etc., Ch.:Value of Beneficence towards Daughters.

Prophet to be distributed in charity, a small grandson of his took one of the dates and put it into his mouth. The Prophet admonished him: "My dear, throw it out, throw it out, know you not that Muhammad's people do not partake of charity?"[14] On another occasion he admonished his daughter Fatima to continue to be diligent in righteous action, pointing out that on the Day of Judgment she would not be asked whose daughter she was, but only how she occupied herself.[15]

The Quran lays great stress on kindness towards neighbours (4:37). The Prophet emphasized on many occasions the duty owed to a neighbour, saying: "So repeatedly and so much has God impressed upon me the duty owed to a neighbour that I began to think that a neighbour might perhaps be named an heir".[16] Urging his companions to keep constantly in mind the need of kindliness toward their neighbours, he pointed out that this was not at all difficult; all that was necessary

[14] Muslim I, Sect.:*Zakat*, Ch.:Prophet's family forbidden to accept Charity.

[15] Bukhari II, Sect.:Admonition, Ch.:Are Wives and Children counted among Close Relations?

[16] Bukhari IV, Sect.:Good Behaviour, Ch.:Benevolence towards Neighbours.

was that one should be willing at all times to share with one's neighbour; even if one has only broth for a meal, it is easy to add an extra cup of water and share the broth with one's neighbour.[17]

In the same way, the needy and the wayfarer must be looked after (4:37). The insistence upon kindness and help to the wayfarer is striking. Only a person who had not bad occasion to travel in foreign lands, where even the language is unfamiliar, can properly appreciate this direc tion. The traveller need not be poor and wanting in means. The mere fact that he is in a strange land, among strange people, and, perhaps, unable to express his needs in their language, should make him an object of kindly and helpful attention. On some occasions it may be a great relief merely to be furnished with directions concerning the road, the situation of a hostelry, or a needed address. All this is part of "kindness to the wayfarer," which is repeatedly enjoined in the Quran.

Those burdened with debt and those held in captivity because they are unable to pay their ransom or to purchase their freedom are proper objects of "spending in the cause of Allah" (9:60).

Orphans have been made the objects of paticular care.

[17] Muslim II, Sec.:Virtue etc., Ch.:Benevolence towards Neighbours.

Their proper upbringing and the due administration of their property must be ensured. Detailed directions are laid down with regard to the guardianship of minors and the administration of their property. It is the duty of the guardian to check up on the upbringing of the orphan from time to time. When the orphan comes of age and if he is of sound judgment, his property should be handed over to him in the presence of witnesses. A guardian or administrator of an orphan's property is entitled to a suitable allowance if he cannot afford to give the time necessary without compensation, but if he is himself in easy circumstances he is not entitled to any compensation (4:7). If the orphan on attaining majority should prove to be of defective judgment, a suitable allowance should be made for his upkeep, and he should be given such advice as he may need, but his property should be duly administered and his interests safeguarded (4:6).

The property of the orphan should not be dealt with to his prejudice by exchange or by being held in common with the property of the guardian (4:3). The Quran reinforces the guardian's obligation towards the minor in very emphatic language. "Let those who deal with minors have the same circumspection in their minds as they would wish for in respect of their own little ones if they were to leave them behind. Let them, therefore, fear Allah and always speak the straightforward word. Those who consume the property of orphans unjustly only swallow fire into their bellies" (4:10-11).

Younger people are admonished to show due respect and consideration for older people, and older people are exhorted to treat younger people with kindness and affection. The Prophet said: "He who does not behave kindly towards younger people and does not show due respect to older ones is not of us".[18]

Islam aims at merging all sections of society into a single community so that all persons may feel themselves to be members of the same family. A whole set of directions exhorts those who are better off to adopt simple ways of life and not to set up artifical barriers in the way of free social intercourse. For instance, the well-to-do are urged towards moderation in food and drink (7:32), and to shun all vanity (23:4). They should be neither stingy, holding back their wealth and substance from being shared by others, nor extravagant, indulging themselves and the members of their families without regard for others who also have a right to share in their wealth (25:58; 51:20). Simple ways of life, dispensing

---

[18] Tirmidhi I, Sect.:Virtue, Ch.:Kindness towards the Young.

with artificial ceremonial, render social intercourse easy and agreeable.

Islam lays great stress on cleanliness of body, clothing, dwellings, public places, and the like (74:5-6). Frequent ablutions and baths are prescribed.

It is recognized that there must be diversity of all kinds in a healthy society, and that it is not only futile but harmful to covet that in which others excel. Each must exercise his or her own capacities and talents and strive to promote both individual and common good. All asking of favours should be from God alone (4:33). Begging is prohibited except in case of extreme need.

Various aspects of good manners are insisted upon. "The true servants of the Gracious One are those who walk in the earth with dignity, and when they are addressed rudely they say:'Peace'" (25:64). "Turn not thy face away from people in pride, nor walk in the earth haughtily; surely Allah loves not any arrogant boaster. Moderate thy pace when walking and soften thy voice when thou speakest" (31:19-20).

The Muslim greeting, which is common throughout the Islamic world, is: "Peace be on you and the mercy of Allah and His blessings." The Quran directs that one should greet one's fellow beings with a better greeting than one receives oneself, or at least return the same

(4:87). One is urged to adopt a straightforward manner of speech and not to equivocate (33:71).

When calling on people or entering one's own house one must go in by the front door, as a matter of courtesy, so as not to take anyone by surprise (2:190); furthermore, when calling on people, one must ask permission before one enters; and when one enters; one should greet the inmates with the salutation of peace (24:28). "If you find no one therein, do not enter until permission is granted to you. If it be said to you, 'Go back,' then go back; that is purer for you. Allah knows well what you do. There is no harm for you to enter freely uninhabited houses wherein are your goods. Allah knows that which you disclose and that which you conceal" (24:29-30).

Before starting on a journey, due provision must be made therefor, to obviate embarrassment (2:198).

Only three types of public associations are approved of. First, those formed for the purpose of promoting the general welfare, in other words, charitable associations and the like. Second, those the object of which is to promote the spread and propagation of knowledge and investigation and research into the sciences, arts, philosophy, etc. Third, those established for the purpose of peaceful settlement of disputes and for removing causes of friction, whether in domestic, national, or international spheres, and thereby promoting peace among mankind (4:115). When people are gathered together for a common purpose, thy should behave in an orderly manner, and should not leave or disperse without permission (24:63). When required to make room in a gathering, this should be done cheerfully, and all directions should be carried out with eagerness (58:12).

All people should behave with dignity, and particular attention must be paid to the maintenance of order in public places and thoroughfares and to keeping them clean. Persons using public places must take care that no undue inconvenience is occasioned to others using the same, nor should any person be exposed to risk or injury. The Prophet said that a person passing through a street carrying anything pointed or with a sharp edge should cover it up, so that nobody is exposed to the risk of injury through his carelessness.[19] He also directed that people should not move from places where an infectious epidemic has broken out to other inhabited places, as this would result in spreading the infection.[20]

The obligation is laid upon everyone to urge others

---

[19] Muslim II, Ch.:He who carries a Weapon, etc.

[20] Muslim II, Sect.:Security, Ch.:Plague, etc.

towards goodness and to seek to restrain them from evil, but with kindness and affection (31:18). Spying, back biting and undue suspicion must be avoided (49:13). Someone asked the Prophet whether it was backbiting to mention a defect or shortcoming from which another did in fact suffer. The Prophet replied that that was exactly what backbiting meant, for if the defect or shortcoming did not in fact exist, the person attributing it to another would be guilty both of slander and of backbiting.[21] If a person has been guilty of slandering another, this must not be communicated to the person slandered, because it would create mischief. The Prophet said that a person who slanders another shoots an arrow at him, which falls by the way, but a person who hears a slander and carries the tale of it to the person slandered is like one who directs the arrow to its mark.[22]

It is the duty of every Muslim constantly to seek increase of knowledge (20:115). The Prophet said that the seeking of knowledge is a duty cast upon every Muslim man and woman,[23] and he went so far as to add

[21] Muslim II, Sect.:Virtue, etc., Ch.:Prohibition of Backbiting.

[22] Ibid.

[23] Ibn Maja I, Sect.:Dignity of the Learned, etc.

"even if it should involve a journey to far-off Cathay",[24] He further said: "A word of wisdom is the lost property of a Muslim. He should seize it wherever he finds it".[25]

With regard to servants, the Prophet said: "They are your brothers. and you should treat them as such. Provide them with the kind of clothes that you wear, and if you set them a hard task, join them in it to help them complete it"[26] He directed that when food is prepared, the person who helped to prepare it should be invited to partake of it.[27]

The wages of a labourer must be paid to him "before the sweat dries upon his body".[28]

The Prophet was very insistent upon kindness towards animals. On one occasion he noticed a dove flying around agitatedly, and discovered that somebody had caught its young. He was very annoyed and asked the person to restore the young to the mother

[24] Baihiqui, on the authority of As-Sayuti I, under letter a p. 37.

[25] Tirmidhi II, Sect.:Knowledge, Ch.:Learning ranks higher than worship.

[26] Abu Daud IV, Sect.:Good Beliaviour, Ch.:Rights of those held in Custody.

[27] Ibid.

[28] Ibn Maja II, Sect.:Pledges, Ch.:Wages of Labourers.

immediately.[29] During a journey he noticed that an ant-heap had been set on fire. He admonished against it.[30] When he saw a donkey that had been branded on the face, he said that this was a cruel practice. If branding be necessary, the Prophet pointed out, it must be done on the leg, where the muscles are not so sensitive. No animal, he added, should be beaten on the face, as the face is the most sensitive part of the body.[31]

Perhaps the most comprehensive direction within the domain of social values is: "Help one another in righteousnes and virtue; but help not one another in sin and transgression" (5:3). When the Prophet said on one occasion, "Go to the help of your brother whether oppressor or oppressed," he was asked, "We understand what is meant by going to the help of a brother who is oppressed, but how shall we help a brother who is an oppressor?" The Prophet replied: "By restraining him from oppressing others".[32]

The Prophet defined a Muslim as "one from whose

---

[29] Abu Daud IV, Sect.:Good Behaviour, Ch.:On Slaughter of Ants.

[30] Ibid.

[31] Muslim II, Sect.:Dress and Adornment, Ch.:Prohibition against beating or branding an animal on its face.

[32] Bukhari II, Sect.:Oppression, Ch.:Help you Brother.

hands and tongue his fellows apprehend no harm"[33] He furnished a strong motive for mutual co-operation and help when he said, "If a person occupies himself in helping his brother, Allah occupies Himslf in helping him".[34]

[33] Bukhari I, Sect.:Faith, Ch.:Muslim, etc.

[34] Tirmidhi II, Sect.:Virtue, etc., Ch.Benevolence, etc.

IV

Economic Values

In the economic sphere the basic concept in Islam is that absolute ownership of everything belongs to God alone (2:108; 3:190). Man is God's vicegerent on earth. God has subjected to man's service "whatsoever is in the heavens and whatsoever is in the earth" (45:14). This has reference to the whole of mankind. "Allah is He Who has appointed you (mankind) His vicegerents in the earth," and he who fails to recognize this dignity and to act in accordance therewith shall be answerable for his neglect and will not only suffer loss but will also incur the displeasure of his Lord (35:40).

Legal ownership of the individual, that is to say the right of possession, enjoyment and transfer of property, is recognized and safeguarded in Islam; but all ownership is subject to the moral obligation that in all wealth all sections of society, and even animals, have a right to share. “In their wealth they acknowledge the right of those who asked and of those who could not” (51:20).

Part of this obligation is given legal form and is made effective through legal sanctions, but the greater part is sought to be secured by voluntary effort put forth out of a desire to achieve the highest moral and spiritual benefits for all concerned. In fact, this supplementing of legal obligations through voluntary effort runs through every part of the Islamic system. Its operation can be observed in every sphere.

The object of the Islamic economic system is to secure the widest and most beneficent distribution of wealth through institutions set up by it and through moral exhortation. Wealth must remain in constant circulation among all sections of the community and should not become the monoply of the rich (59:8).

Islam recognizes the diversity of capacities and talents, which is in itself beneficent, and consequently the diversity in earnings and material rewards (4:33). It does not approve of a dead-level equality in the distribution of wealth, as that would defeat the very purpose of the diversity, and would amount to denying “the favour of Allah” (16:72). It is obvious that if the incentive of proportionate reward for labour, effort, skill and talent were to be removed, not only would initiative and enterprise be adversely affected, but intellectual progress would also be arrested. That is why the theoretical doctrine of equal reward irrespective of the diversity of skill, capacities and talents that have gone into the production of wealth has never been maintained for long, even where it has been proclaimed as State policy, and has had to be modified through recourse to various devices designed to secure diversity in reward. On the other hand, Islam does not leave the principle of competition and of proportionate rewards to work itself out mechanically; that too would lead to hardship and injustice, and would retard the moral and spiritual development of individuals and of society as a whole.

The principal economic obligation is the pavment of the capital levy called *Zakat* (22:79; 23:5). The word *Zakat* means "that which purifies" and "that which fosters." All original sources of wealth-the sun, the moon, the stars the clouds that bring rain, the winds that drive the clouds and carry the pollen, all phenomena of nature-are the gifts; of God to the whole of mankind. Wealth is produced by the appliction of man's skill and labour to the resources which God has provided for man's subsistence and comfort and over part of which man enjoys proprietary rights, to the extent recognized by Islam. In the wealth that is produced, therefore, three parties are entitled to share: the workman, whether skilled or unskilled; the person who supplies the capital; and the community as representing mankind. The community's share in produced wealth is called *Zakat*. After this has been set aside for the benefit of the community, the rest is "purified" and may be divided beween the remaining parties that are entitled to share in it.

The *Zakat* is assessed on both capital and income, Its incidence varies with reference to different kinds of property, but on the average it works out at two and one half per cent of the capital value. The proceeds of the *Zakat* are devoted towards relieving poverty and distress, winning over the cheerful co-operation of those who have net yet completely adjusted their lives to the Islamic system, providing ransom for prisoners of war, helping those in debt, providing comfort and convenience for travellers, supplying capital where talent is available but funds are lacking, providing stipends for scholars and research workers, meeting the expenses involved in collecting and administering the *Zakat*, and generally towards all things beneficial for the community as a whole, such as public health, public works, medical services, and educational institutions (9:60). It thus "fosters" the welfare of the community (9:103).

Besides the *Zakat*, which was described by the Prophet as "a levy imposed upon the well-to-do which is returned to the poorer section of the people",[35] implying that it is their just due and must be paid back to them, there are other institutions within the economic sphere operating constantly to further the objective of the whole system. One of these is the Islamic system of inheritance and succession. Under this system a person may not dispose of more than one-third of his property by testamentary directions. While he is in the enjoyment of normal health he may dispose of his property freely, subject, of course, to the moral obligations, some of which have been noted; but neither by will nor by gift, once he enters upon a stage of illness which terminates in death, may he dispose of more than the permitted one-third. By such disposition he may provide legacies for friends, for servants, and for charity.

The rest of the inheritance must be divided among prescribed heirs in specified shares. No part of the one-third permitted to be disposed of by will may be used to

[35] Bukhari I, Sect.:*Zakat*, Ch.:Obligation of *Zakat*.

augment the share of one or more heirs to the prejudice of the remaining heirs. Each heir can take only his or her prescribed share and no more; nor can any heir be deprived of the whole or any part of his or her share. Their is a wide circle of heirs. If a person should die leaving father, mother, wife or husband, sons and daughters, each is an heir and is entitled to a determined share of the inheritance. In some cases the share of a female heir in the same degree of relationship to the deceased as a male heir is equal to that of the male heir, but normally it is one half of that of a male heir in the same degree (4:8, 12-13).

The difference between the normal share of female heirs and male heirs in the same degree of relationship to the deceased is not in fact discriminatory to the prejudice of the female heirs. Under the Islamic system, the obligation of maintaining the family always rests upon the husband, even when, as is often the case, the wife's personal income may be larger than the husband's. To enable the male to discharge his obligations towards the family, his share in the inheritance is twice that of a female in the same degree of relationship as himself. Far from operating to the prejudice of the female heir, this actually places her in a favourable position as compared with the male heir, because she does not have financial obligations to the family.

Thus the Islamic system of inheritance operates to distribute wealth so that a large number of people may have a competence or, at least, a little, rather than that one or a few should have a large share and the rest nothing. As if all this left something to be desired, the exhortation is added: "If other relations, who are not included among the heirs, and orphans and the poor be present at the division of the inheritance, bestow something upon them therefrom and speak to them words of kindness" (4:9).

Another major provision is the prohibition against the making of loans on interest. The word used in this connection in the Quran is *riba*, the connotation of which is not identical with that of the word "interest" as commonly understood; but for the present purpose "interest" may be used as a rough equivalent. *Riba* is prohibited because it tends to draw wealth into the hands of a small circle and to restrict the exercise of beneficence towards one's fellow beings. In the case of loans which bear interest, the lender in effect takes advantage of, and makes a profit out of, the need or distress of another. Islam urges the making of loans, but says they should be beneficent loans, meaning without interest. If the debtor finds himself in straitened circumstances when the time for repayment of the loan arrives, he should be granted respite till his circumstances improve, but "if you remit it altogether as charity, that shall be the better for you, if only you knew" (2:281).

It is a mistake to imagine that transactions involving interest bring about an increase in the national wealth. The Quran says that in the sight of Allah it is not a beneficent increase. "But whatever you give in *Zakat*, seeking the favour of Allah-it is these who will increase their wealth manifold" (20:40).

Trade, commercial partnerships, co-operatives, joint stock companies are all legitimate activities and operations (2:276). Islam does, however, lay down regulations with regard to commercial activities, designed to secure that they be carried on honestly and beneficently. All contracts, whether involving large amounts or small, must be reduced to writing, setting out all the terms thereof, as "this is more likely to keep out doubts, and avoid disputes" (2:283). The writing should set out the terms agreed upon fairly, and as a further precaution it is laid down that the terms of the contract shall be dictated by the person who undertakes the liability. If the person on whose behalf the liability is undertaken is a minor, or of unsound judgment, then his guardian or the person representing his interests should dictate the terms of the contract (2:283).

Monopolies and the cornering of commodities are prohibited; so also is the holding back of produce from the market in expectation of a rise in prices.[36] All this is opposed to beneficence, and those who indulge in such practices seek to take advantage of the need or distress of their fellow beings. The seller is under obligation to disclose any defect in the article offered for sale.[37] Goods and commodities for sale should go into the open market, and the seller or his agent must be aware of the state of the market before proposals are made for purchase of the goods or commodities in bulk. He should not be taken unawares, lest advantage be taken of bis ignorance of the state of the market and the prevailing prices.[38]

There are stern injunctions in the Quran with regard to the giving of full weight and measure (26:182-185). "Woe unto those who give short measure; those who,

---

36 Ibn Maja II, Sect.:Trade, Ch.:Holding back Commodities; Muslim II; Sect.:Sales, Ch.:Prohibition of holding back Foodstuffs.

37 Bukhari II, Sect.:Sales, Ch.:Revocation, etc., Ibn Maja II. Sect.:trade, Ch.:Seller should disclose defects.

38 Bukhari II, Sect.:Sales, Ch.:Prohibition against purchase of goods before they arrive in the market.

when they take by measure from other people, take it full, but when they give by measure to others or weigh out to them, they give them less. Do not such people know that they will be raised again unto a terrible day, the day when mankind will stand before the Lord of the worlds?" (82:2-7).

Defective or worthless goods or articles should not be given in exchange for good ones (4:3). In short, any kind of transaction which does not comply with the highest standards of honesty and integrity must be eschewed, "for God loves not the dishonest" (8:59).

Gambling is prohibited, inasmuch as it promotes dissension and hatred and tends to deter those who indulge in it from the remembrance of God and from Prayer, thus occasioning a great deal more harm than any possible benefit that may be derived from it (2:220; 5:92). It also brings sudden and undeserved accession of wealth and encourages extravagance. Indulgence in gambling often brings ruin and misery in its wake.

All unlawful means of acquiring property are prohibited, as these in the end destroy a people (4:30). Acquisition of property or goods through falsehood falls in the same category. It is equally unlawful to seek to establish a title to property by obtaining judgment through corrupt means like bribery or false evidence

(2:189). The Prophet said that a party to a dispute which obtains a judgment in its favour, knowing that it is not in the right, only collects a quantity of fire for itself and not something from which it can draw any benefit.[39]

On the other hand, goods and property lawfully acquired are a bounty of God which is provided by Him as a means of support. They should be properly looked after and should not be wasted through neglect. A person of defective judgment should not be permitted to squander away his substance. It should be managed and administered for him, and provision should be made for his maintenance out of the income (4:6).

Niggardliness is condemned as a negative and destructive quality. While, on the one hand, ostentation and vanity are disapproved of, on the other, it is not considered right that a person who is well off should pretend to be poor, fearing lest he be called upon to help others. By doing this he makes himself poor in effect, and deprives himself of the benefits that may be derived from God's bounty (4:38). The wealth of misers, instead of bringing them any advantage, becomes a handicap and arrests their moral and spiritual development (3:181). The other extreme, extravagance, is equally

[39] Bukhari IV, Sect.: Judgments, Ch.: Admonition to Parties.

condemned. Even when giving to, or sharing with, others a person should not go so far as to render himself in tum an object of charity (17:30). Hoarding is absolutely prohibited because it puts wealth out of circulation and deprives the owner as well as the rest of the community of its beneficent use (9:34). The truth is that God alone is All-Sufficient, and all prosperity proceeds from Him. It is men who are in need, and prosperity is achieved not through miserliness or holding back, but through beneficent spending, which is spending "in the cause of Allah," namely, in the service of His creatures (47:39).

As already stated, a legal owner of property is not the only person entitled to its use. Those in need who ask, and even those who do not ask or are unable to express their need, have a right in the property of those who are better off, inasmuch as all wealth is a bounty of God and is acquired through the use of resources which God has provided for the benefit of the whole of mankind (51:20). That is why the Quran directs that kindred, the needy, the wayfarer, must be paid their due (30:39). To this end there is emphatic and repeated exhortation in the Quran. Such giving should be in proportion to the need of the person to be helped and in accord with the means of the giver, and should not proceed from any expectation of receiving a return (17:27; 74:7).

It is indeed the highest bounty of God that He should have endowed man with appropriate faculties and capacities and then subjected the universe to man's beneficent service to enable him to achieve the fullest development of his faculties in every sphere of life. Yet some people, instead of putting their faculties to beneficent use in the service of their fellow beings and spending that which they possess for the same purpose, have a tendency to hold back, not realizing that even from the purely selfish point of view the greatest benefit is to be derived from beneficent spending and not from parsimonious holding back. This is the fundamental principle which is the basis of all prosperity, individual, national and universal. The Quran emphasizes this repeatedly. For instance: "Behold, you are those who are favoured by being called upon to spend in the way of Allah; but of you there are some who hold back, yet whoso holds back does so only to his own prejudice. It is Allah Who is All-Sufficient, and it is you who are needy" (47:38). Holding back renders a person progressively poorer in the true sense, inasmuch as he stultifies his faculties, and by putting that which he possesses out of service and out of circulation, renders it completely barren and unfruitful.

The subject of charitable and beneficent spending

has so many aspects that they can be better appreciated in the juxtaposition in which the Quran puts them. The following excerpts contain a whole philosophy of spending, giving and sharing, on which no detailed commentary is called for:

> "The case of those who spend their wealth for the cause of Allah is like that of a grain of corn which grows seven ears, in each ear a hundred grains. Allah multiplies even more for whomsoever He pleases. Allah is Bountiful, All-Knowing.
>
> "They who spend their wealth for the cause of Allah, then follow not up what they have spent with reproach or injury, for them is their reward with their Lord, and they shall have no fear, nor shall they grieve.
>
> "A kind word and forgiveness are better than charity followed by injury. Allah is All-Sufficient, Forbearing.
>
> "O ye who believe, render not vain your charity by taunt and injury, like him who spends his wealth to be seen of men, and he believes not in Allah and the Last Day. His case is like that of a smooth rock covered with earth, on which heavy rain falls, leaving it bare and hard. They shall not secure the benefit of aught of what they earn ...

"The likeness of those who spend their wealth to seek the pleasure of Allah and to strengthen their souls is that of a garden on elevated ground. Heavy rain falls on it so that it brings forth its fruit twofold, and if heavy rain does not fall on it, then light rain suffices. Allah sees what you do.

"Does any one of you desire that there should be for him a garden of palm trees and vines with streams flowing beneath it, and with all kinds of fruit for him therein-while old age has stricken him and he has helpless offspring-and that a fiery whirlwind should smite it and it be all consumed? Thus does Allah make His Signs clear to you that you may ponder.

"O ye who believe, spend of the pure things that you have earned, and of what We bring forth for you from the earth; and seek not what is bad to spend out of it when you would not receive it yourselves except with closed eyes. Know that Allah is All-Sufficient, Praiseworthy.

"Satan threatens you with poverty and enjoins upon you what is foul, whereas Allah promises you forgiveness from Himself, and Bounty. Allah is Bountiful, All-Knowing.

"If you give alms openly, it is well; but if you keep

them secret and give them to the poor, it is better for you. He will remove from you many of your ills. Allah is aware of what you do ...

> "Whatever wealth you spend, it is to the benefit of your own selves, while you spend not but to seek the favour of Allah. Whatever of wealth you spend, it shall be paid back to you in full and you shall not be wronged.
>
> "Charity is for the needy, who are restricted in the cause of Allah and are unable to move about in the land. The ignorant person thinks them to be free from want because of their abstaining from asking. You shall know them by their appearance; they do not ask of men with importunity. Whatever of wealth you spend, surely Allah has perfect knowledge thereof.
>
> "Those who spend their wealth by night and day, secretly and openly, have their reward with their Lord, on them shall come no fear, nor shall they grieve" (2:262-269, 272-275)

V

Islam and the Declaration: The Preamble

The Preamble of the Declaration recalls in general terms the values and purposes which the Declaration is designed to secure and the methods through which they might be secured.

The preceding sections have drawn attention to some of these values as being part of those that Islam seeks to inculcate and establish. These and some others will be considered in somewhat greater detail with reference to the specific articles of the Declaration. So far as the Preamble is concerned it should be enough to point out that Islam lays the duty of constantly promulgating Islamic values upon every individual Muslim. The generic word for these values is *ma'roof*, meaning that which is good, equitable, desirable. "You are the best people, for you have been raised for the good of mankind, you enjoin what is equitable [ma'roof] and forbid evil and believe in Allah" (3:111). "Let there be among you a body of persons who should invite to goodness, and enjoin equity [ma'roof] and forbid evil. It is they who shall prosper" (3:t05).

It is characteristic of the Quran that it accords generous recognition to merit wherever it finds it. In the present context it refers to peoples who believe in other scriptures in these terms: "They are not all alike. Among the People of the Book there is a party who stand by their covenant, they recite the word of Allah in the hours of night and prostrate themselves before Him.

"They believe in Allah and the Last Day, and enjoin what is good [*ma'roof*] and forbid evil, and hasten, vying with one another, towards the doing of good. These are among the righteous.

"Whatever they do, they shall not be denied its due reward. Allah well knows the God-fearing" (3:114-116).

Articles 1 and 2

These article stress the freedom, equality and dignity of man. Being endowed with reason and conscience, men should act towards one another in a spirit of brotherhood. No discrimination should be practised or permitted in respect of any.

The Quran stresses the equality of mankind as deriving from the Unity of its common Creator, Who created man of one species and to Whom all men owe allegiance and obedience. "O mankind, worship your Lord Who created you and those who were before you, that you may become righteous; Who made the earth a bed for you, and the heaven a roof, and caused water to come down from the clouds and therewith brought forth fruits for your sustenance" (2:22-23). All are His creatures and all are entitled to partake of His bounties. "O mankind, be mindful of their physical origin as being of the same species. There is no room for any claim of superiority in respect of origin or descent.

This matter of common origin is stressed as a Divine favour. "Allah has made for you mates from among yourselves, and has made for you, from your mates, children and grandchildren, and has provided you with good things. Will they then run after vanity and deny the favour of Allah?" (16:73).

Islam concedes no privilege on account of birth, nationality or any other factor. True nobility proceeds from righteousness alone. "O mankind, We have created you from male and female, and we have made you into tribes and sub-tribes for greater facility of intercourse. Verily, the most honoured from among you in the sight of Allah is he who is the most righteous among you. Surely, Allah is All-Knowing, All-Aware" (49:14).

God has conferred upon man a position of great dignity by appointing mankind as His "vicegerents in the earth" (35:40), equipping man with appropriate faculties and capacities, among them hearing, sight, understanding, and constraining to his service the Universe, which is governed by law and is wholly beneficent. "Surely, We have created man in the best mould" (95:5).

"Such is the Knower of the unseen and the seen, the Mighty, the Merciful. Who has made perfect everything. He has created. He began the creation of man from clay. Then he made his progeny from an extract of an insignificant fluid. Then He fashioned him and breathed into him of His spirit. He has bestowed on you hearing and sight and understanding. But little thanks do you give" (32:7-10).

"He has constrained to your service whatever is in the heavens and whatsoever is in the earth; all of it is from Him. In that surely are Signs for a people who reflect" (45:14).

Man is aware of all this and is a witness against his

own self, though he may put forward his excuses (75:15-16), for he has been equipped with a lively conscience, with a sharp, self-accusing faculty that continues to admonish him (75:3).

The spirit of brotherhood is emphasized at every turn in Islam and permeates every section of Muslim society. It is the practical expression of the truth that all men are creatures and servants of the same Beneficent Creator and must for His sake, and for the purpose of winning His pleasure, live together as brethren.

"Hold fast, all together, by the rope of Allah and be not divided; and remember the favour of Allah which He bestowed upon you when you were enemies and He united your hearts in love so that by His grace you became as brethren; and you were on the brink of a pit of fire and He saved you from it. Thus does Allah explain to you His Commandments that you may be guided" (3:104).

The Prophet admonished: "Be not envious of another, nor bear ill-will nor cut off relations with another; behave towards one another as brethren, O servants of Allah".[40] He reminded: "You are as brothers, one to another, so let no one transgress against another,

[40] Bukhari IV, Sect.:Good Behaviour.

nor leave another to endure transgression unaided. Remember, that he who occupies himself in assisting his brother will find Allah coming to his own assistance, and he who strives to relieve his brother of anxiety will find himself shielded against anxiety by Allah on the Day of Judgment, and he who overlooks his brother's fault will find his own faults overlooked by Allah".[41]

He observed: "None of you can be a believer unless he should desire for his brother what he desires for himself".[42]

He urged: "Go to the help of your brother whether he is an oppressor or is oppressed." On being asked how an oppressor may be helped, he rejoined, "Stop him from continuing in his course of oppression".[43]

Article 3

This is a general article which embodies what has come to be regarded as a truism. Several of the articles that follow spell out some of the specific elements of

[41] Tirmidhi II, Sect.:Virtue, etc., Ch.:Benevolence.

[42] Bukhari I, Sect., Faith, Ch .. It is part of faith to desire for one's brother what one desires for oneself.

[43] Bukhari II, Sect.:Oppression, Ch.:Help your Brother.

"the right to life, liberty and security of person." Islam is as emphatic as any other system in safeguarding these rights. Suicide is forbidden (4:30) and also infanticide (17:32). Accountability in respect of infanticide is stressed in awe-inspiring terms (81:9-10).

The sense of horror sought to be inspired against destroying human life may be gathered from: "Wherefore We prescribed for the children of Israel that whosoever killed a person-unless it be for killing a person or for creating disorder in the land-it shall be as if he had slaughtered all mankind; and whoso secures the life of one, it shall be as if he had secured the life of all mankind" (5:33).

The specific prohibition is also clear: "Say: Come, I will rehearse to you what your Lord has enjoined: that you associate not anything as partner with Him and that you comport yourselves benevolently towards your parents, and that you kill not your children for fear of poverty-it is We Who provide for you and for them-and that you approach not nigh unto indecency, whether overt or hidden; and that you destroy not the life that Allah has made sacred, save by right. That is what He has enjoined upon you, that you may understand.

"Approach not the property of an orphan, except in a way that is beneficent, till he attains his maturity. Give full measure and weight with equity. We ask not any soul except according to its capacity. When you speak be just, even if the person concerned be a relative, and fulfil the covenant of Allah. That is what He enjoins upon you that you may be mindful" (6:152-153).

A more comprehensive injunction is directed against all evil thoughts and designs, all manner of churlish behaviour and every form of trespass, whether against the person, property, honour or good name of another (16:91).

In his Farewell Address the Prophet admonished: "Your persons, properties and honour are declared sacred like the sanctity attaching to this day, this month and this spot. Let them not be violated." He was speaking on the occasion of the Pilgrimage, to the host of pilgrims gathered in the Plain of 'Arafat. When he concluded his Address he charged those who were present and had heard him to convey what he had said to those who could not be present: "Perchance, one who is not present here may be even more mindful than one who is".[44]

In pursuance of his charge, very wide publicity continues to be given to the comprehensive Address

[44] Hanbal V, p. 411.

delivered by him on that occasion, which is looked upon as his Testament.

Article 4

This article is designed to secure the abolition of slavery and all forms of servitude, wherever they might still persist.

The historical treatment of the institution of slavery does not pertain to our present thesis. But it is necessary, for the proper appreciation of the attitude of Islam towards slavery, to cast a cursory glance at the incidence of this ancient institution as it flourished in pre-Islamic Arabia, and then to consider to what degree Islam sought to eliminate, modify or reform it.

In pre-Islamic Arabia slavery flourished unchecked and the lot of the slave was miserable in the extreme. The master possessed and exercised the power of life and death over the slave. That this was so everywhere did not make it any more endurable for those who were subjected to its rigours.

One source of recruitment into the ranks of those held in bondage was capture in war or in tribal raids. Prisoners of war were in no better case. Those who were not exchanged or ransomed were generally put to the sword, but if spared, were held in slavery.

Islam prohibited slave-driving raids altogether, made aggressive war unlawful, improved out of recognition the lot of prisoners of war taken in defensive fighting by instituting regulations which should secure not only humane but civilized and liberal treatment of them, and set up values and standards which, if they had been persisted in, would have secured the abolition of the institution of slavery within a comparatively short period.

The Prophet's own attitude towards slavery is well-known. After his marriage with Khadeejah, who was wealthy in her own right, while the Prophet (the event took place fifteen years before he received the Divine call) owned practically nothing at all, she placed all that she owned at his disposal. He distributed the greater part of her property to the poor and freed all her slaves. One young man, Zaid, chose voluntarily to stay with him and to serve him. After a time his father and uncle tracked him to Mecca and offered to purchase his freedom. The Prophet explained that Zaid was free and could go with them if he so wished, and that there was no question of any payment. Zaid, however, refused to go with them pointing out to them that he was much happier where he was than he would be at home with his parents.

Later, the Prophet procured the hand of his first cousin Zainab b. Jahsh, for Zaid, though the marriage did not prove lasting and ended in divorce. Zaid, however, continued to be a devoted follower of the Prophet and suffered martyrdom like so many others in the cause of Islam. After Zaid's death the Prophet continued to bestow deep affection on his son, Usamah. During the time of 'Umar, the second Khalifah, his son, Abdullah, once asked his father why the latter had rated Usamah higher than Abdullah in a particular case, despite the fact that he had served Islam with greater distinction than had Usamah. "For the reason, son, that Usamah's father and Usamah were dearer to the Prophet than thy father and thee," was the reply of 'Umar!

Throughout his life the Prophet never owned any slave, as the institution of slavery and anything savouring of it were repugnant to him.

But the conditions of contemporary life (it was the beginning of the seventh century after Christ) did not permit a total elimination of the exercise of control by one human being over another, though the degree and incidence of such control were so regulated by Islam as to render it very light and easily endurable, if not entirely beneficent in all cases. In view of the deterioration that subsequently set in, it may not be without profit to examine somewhat more closely the changes and regulations instituted by Islam.

It may be broadly stated that in Islam such control had its origin in war.

During the Meccan period (610-622), the Prophet and his small band of devoted followers had borne the contempt and scorn of the Quraish, and later, cruel and sustained persecution at the hands of the latter, with dignified and steadfast fortitude. Under every kind of provocation they maintained their role and attitude of peaceful and lawabiding citizens, under the rule of a sort of oligarchy composed of the heads of the principal families of the Quraish. When the Prophet was forced to leave Mecca and moved to Medina (the majority of his male followers having already arrived there) his advent (622) was acclaimed not only by the Muslims (both those who had arrived from Mecca and those who were residents of Medina) but also by the non-Muslim Arabs and the Jews. They soon agreed to accept him as Chief of Medina, and a charter was drawn up which made provision for the regulation of the affairs of the city.

But peace was denied to the Prophet and the Muslims even in Medina. The Meccans first demanded that he should be returned to them, and when this demand was turned down they started preparations for leading a strong force against Medina to compel his surrender.

It was in this contingency that the Muslims were accorded Divine permission to take up arms in defence of freedom of conscience.

"Permission to fight is granted to those against whom war is made, because they have been wronged-and Allah indeed has power to help them-those who have been driven out of their homes unjustly only because they said 'Our Lord is Allah'. If Allah did not repel some men by means of others, there would surely have been pulled down cloisters and churches and synagogues and mosques, wherein the name of Allah is oft commemorated, Allah will surely help him who helps Him. Allah is indeed Powerful, Mighty. This permission has been granted to those who, if We establish them in the earth, will observe Prayer and pay the *Zakat* and enjoin equity and forbid evil. With Allah rests the final issue of all affairs" (22:40-42).

Thus fighting is permissible only to repel or halt aggression; but even in the course of such fighting, Muslims are not permitted to adopt unduly aggressive measures. "Fight in the cause of Allah against those who fight against you, but do not transgress. Surely, Allah loves not the transgressors" (2:191). "Persecution is worse than killing" (2:192), for it seeks to destroy the soul, therefore "fight them until there is no persecution, and religion is freely professed for the sake of Allah; but if they desist, then remember that no hostility is allowed except against the aggressors" (2:194).

These are basic and fundamental directives. There is a host of other directions in the Quran with regard to the prosecution of war, but they are all subject to the conditions here laid down, and must be so construed.

Prisoners could only be taken in actual fighting during the course of a justified war. Tribal raids were not permitted, nor could prisoners be taken in scouting skirmishes or chance encounters. "It does not behove a Prophet that he should have captives until he engages in regular fighting in the land. You desire the goods of this world, while Allah desires for you the Hereafter. Allah is Mighty Wise" (8:68).

No regular forces were maintained during the time of the Prophet. Whenever the need arose an *ad hoc* force was assembled and everyone who joined had to provide everything for himself-mount, food, water, arms, etc. No payment was made, except by way of compensation out of spoils gained on the field of battle, e.g. arms, armour, camels, horses and the ransom paid for prisoners of war. Those not exchanged or ransomed were allotted to those who had taken part in the fighting or who were otherwise entitled to compensation, and were put to work. In many cases prisoners of war were released without exchange or ransom as a matter of favour (47:5). Ransom could be very light. After the battle of Badr, it was announced that the ransom of a literate prisoner would be that he should teach the alphabet to ten Muslim children.[45]

Those who could be put to work were entitled to be set at large to work on there own, if they so desired, and to ransom themselves out of their earnings. They could obtain a writing to that effect and were to be helped in carrying out the obligation thus undertaken (24:34).

Those who were fit for marriage were free to marry. "If they be poor, Allah will grant them means out of His bounty. Allah is Bountiful, All-Knowing. Those who find no means of marriage should keep themselves chaste until Allah grants them means out of His bounty" (24:33-34).

Out of the proceeds of the *Zakat*, charitable funds and the income of charitable endowments, provision should be made for ransoming captives and the relief of debtors (9:60).

---

[45] Mirza Bashir Ahmad: Sirat Khataman Nabiyyin II, p. 160, on the authority of Tabaqat Ibn Sa'ad.

All these provisions and devices were designed to facilitate the progressive setting at large of prisoners held in captivity in consequence of their participation in one of the gravest and most heinous moral crimes, namely the attempt, by the use of force, to deprive others of their most precious freedom, the freedom of conscience. They had sought to enslave the souls of others; their just recompense was a partial restriction of their physical liberty, for a term that might prove to be long or short, depending on circumstances and contingencies. During that term, the conditions under which they were held were not too severe. The Prophet had admonished: "These are your brethren over whom Allah has granted you authority, then he who has a brother under his authority should feed him on what he eats himself, should clothe him as he clothes himself, should not set him a task beyond his capacity, and if he is assigned something heavy or difficult, should help him in carrying it out".[46]

On one occasion he observed while passing along, that a man had raised his arm to strike another who was in his custody. "What art thou about?" called out the

[46] Abu Daud IV. Sect.:Good Behaviour, Ch.:Rights of those held in Custody.

Prophet. "Knowest not that Allah has more authority over thee than thou hast over this creature of His?" The man had not been aware that the Prophet was anywhere near, but hastened to respond: "Messenger of Allah, I set him free." "Thou dost well," rejoined the Prophet, .. else thou wouldst have put thyself within reach of the Fire"[47]

The testimony of such prisoners themselves is available that, on occasion, their captors went hungry so that the prisoners might be fed, or that the former walked so that the latter might ride.[48]

When, during the time of 'Umar, the second Khalifah, Jerusalem offered to surrended on condition that the Khalifah should come in person to settle the terms and to take over the city, 'Umar proceeded on the journey from Medina to Jerusalem, accompanied by one such prisoner and taking only one camel, which also carried their meagre food supplies. 'Umar arranged that out of consideration for the animal they should ride it stage by stage by turns. For the last stage it was the tum of the prisoner to ride. He offered to forego his tum, but 'U

---

[47] Ibid.

[48] Sirat Ibn Hisham II, p. 234; Sir William Muir, Life of Muhammad, p. 242.

mar insisted that the arrangement must be adhered to. Thus they arrived in Jerusalem, where the notables and the population were assembled to welcome the great Khalifah, and saw the Khalifah leading the solitary camel ridden by his "slave"![49]

It will thus be seen that Islam aimed at the elimination of slavery and bondage, and instituted regulations and means towards the achievement of that purpose. With the firm establishment of freedom of conscience for everybody the major source of conflict would be removed, and war, which Islam regards as an abnormal and destructive activity, to which recourse should be had only in the last resort, would be abolished. The Quran describes war as a conflagration, and declares that it is God's purpose to put out such a conflagration whenever it erupts. "Whenever they kindle a fire for war, Allah extinguishes it. They strive to create disorder in the earth, and Allah loves not those who create disorder" (5:65). With the abolition of war the only source of such bondage as Islam countenanced would become obsolete and even that mild form of bondage would disappear.

History took a different course. To that we shall

[49] Prof. Abdul Qadir, History of Islam, Vol. I.

revert later. Suffice it to affirm here that the spirit and purpose of Article 4 of the Universal Declaration of Human Rights are in accord with the Islamic objective. In fact, throughout the largest part of the Islamic world the institution of slavery has been progressively abolished; its last vestiges, where they have persisted, are on the way out and it has no chance of being revived anywhere.

Article 5

This article is directed against torture, cruelty, inhuman or degrading treatment or punishment.

So far as treatment is concerned, as Islam does not recognize any basis of discrimination, all persons are entitled to fair and equal treatment; and dignified behaviour and deportment and respect for the dignity of others have been outstanding characteristics of Islamic society even during what might be described as its period of decline.

The Prophet constantly admonished people to behave with calmness and dignity in all situations, and emphasized the need of exercizing courtesy and dignity towards all.

He told the leader of the deputation from the Abdul

Qais tribe: "You have two qualities which are very acceptable to Allah: forbearance and deliberation".[50]

He told his wife Ayesha: "Whatever is done with grace enhances its value, and that which lacks grace loses all value".[51]

He prohibited all cruelty and torture. He said: "No one should be subjected to chastisement by fire",[52] and also admonished against hitting any person on the face.[53]

He noticed a donkey which had been branded on its face, and admonished against the practice. If branding becomes necessary it should be carried out on a less sensitive part of the body.[54]

In the realm of penal law, certain penalties might appear to be severe or even harsh. This is not the occasion to embark upon the relative merit and

---

[50] Muslim I, Sect.:Faith, Ch.:Commandment to believe in Allah and His Messenger.

[51] Muslim II, Sect.:Virtue, etc., Ch.:Value and Grace.

[52] Bukhari II, Sect.:Jehad and Expeditions, Ch.:Prohibition of Chastisement of Allah.

[53] Muslim II, Sect.:Virtue, etc., Ch.:Prohibitin of hitting on the face.

[54] Muslim II, Sect.:Dress and Adornment, Ch.:Prohibition against beating or branding an animal on its face.

usefulness of different types of punishment. One or two considerations might, however, be set down as relevant in this context.

Imprisonment as a penalty for offences, and the establishment of prisons and all their attendant paraphernalia, were comparatively unknown in the world of early Islam, and it is a debatable question even today whether a term of imprisonment is preferable in all cases and situations to, say, a flogging.

The Quran prescribes flogging for certain offences, e.g. fornication or adultery whether on the part of a male or a female (24:3) and slanderous accusation of unchastity against a woman (24:5). The severity of the penalty prescribed for these offences will be more readily appreciated if it is remembered that the safeguarding of moral values and standards is among the primary concerns of religion. Such appreciation, however, is not so easily forthcoming in those sophisticated modem societies in which unchastity on the part of men is considered only a normal manifestation of virility and even on the part of a woman is no longer looked upon with serious disfavour. A Superintendent of Education has recently announced that he does not regard premarital sexual intercourse as morally objectionable in the case of senior school students, and Deans of Universities, though perturbed at the prevalence of sexual relations between college students, profess themselves helpless in face of the situation, particularly, as one of them has observed, when parents themselves not only see no harm in it but encourage it. Every society is entitled to set up and follow its own standards. Islam regards these offences as most heinous and injurious in their consequences. "Come not even nigh unto adultery; surely it is a foul thing and an evil way" (17:33). "Verily, those who slander chaste, unwary, believing women are cursed in this world and the Hereafter and for them is a grievous chastisement" (24:24).

It would be amusing, were it not a matter so grave, that those who erroneously attribute to woman a position of inferiority in Islamic society, themselves hold a woman's honour so cheap that a trespass against it is deemed to be sufficiently atoned for by the payment of monetary compensation to the husband, in the case of adultery, and as used to be the case under the Common Law, to the father in the case of fornication which resulted in pregnancy and thus occasioned loss of service to the father. These are not, however, matters to which a uniform yard-stick can be made applicable. It is submitted that certain types of offences call for severe chastisement, and flogging in the case of such offences cannot be regarded as cruel, inhuman or degrading.

There is one other offence- theft- which Islam classifies as one calling for a severe penalty. In this case the penalty is "cutting off of hands" (5:39). This sounds harsh, but there are several mitigating considerations which should be kept in mind. In the first place it has been uniformly held that the penalty is attracted only in extreme and hardened cases. To attract the extreme penalty, there must be an element of aggravation in the offence committed. The slightest element of extenuation would procure relief for an offender. 'Umar, the second Khalifah, was always on the look-out for any such element, so as to reduce or modify the penalty, and cases so dealt with by him became precedents for those who followed.

In the next place it is worth recalling that in England, for instance, theft of property worth more than a shilling was classified as felony and, like every other felony, was punished with death, up to as late as 1861.

That, however, may not furnish much comfort to the humanist of today. But there is an element of comfort in the situation. It is true that the Arabic expression in the Quran, which literally construed means "cut off their hands", was so construed in early and medieval times. In modern times in most Islamic States a term of imprisonment has been substituted and the literal "cutting off" of hands is exacted in few States and in rare cases. For this, jurists and scholars have found justification in canons of interpretation. Even at the very outset "both hands" (the term employed in the text) were not cut off for a single aggravated offence, though that would be the strict literal meaning of the expression. The use of the plural where the singular was by common accord taken to be meant, furnishes a clue to the secondary meaning of the expression. The term *aidee* (hands) has both a primary (physical) connotation and a secondary one. For instance, Abraham, Isaac and Jacob are described as "possessing hands and eyes" (38:46), which obviously means "possessed of power and vision". *Aidee* (hands), therefore, might well connote strength or capacity.

Qat'a (cutting off) has also a secondary connotation i.e. circumscribing the use of. For instance *qat' a al lisan* (cutting off of the tongue) means imposing silence upon, or circumscribing or prohibiting the use of speech.

Thus "cutting off hands" would have the secondary connotation, circumscribing their capacity or activity, or prohibiting their free movement.

In this context the following examples of the use of *qat' a* or its derivatives may be of interest.

"Those who break the covenant of Allah after having established it, and cut asunder what Allah has bidden to be joined" (2:28), meaning, those who are not mindful of the ties of kinship.

"Would you then, if you are placed in authority, create disorder in the land and cut off your wombs" (47:23), that is to say, sever your ties of kinship?

"This building of theirs, which they have built, will ever continue to be a source of disquiet in their hearts, unless their hearts be cut to pieces" (9:110), that is to say, till their hearts become incapable of feeling.

Of the people of Lot it is said, "Do you indeed come lustfully to men and cut off the highway?" (29:30), that is to say, destroy its security and thus make it unsafe for travellers.

Even when *qat'a* is used in the literal sense, it does not necessarily mean complete severing. It is said of the women of Egypt, "When they saw him (Joseph) they thought highly of him and cut their hands [*qatta'na aidceahunna*] and said, 'Allah be glorified'" (12:32), and when Joseph was summoned to the presence of the King he said to the messenger, "'Go back to thy lord and ask him how fare the women who cut their hands'" (12:51).

Articles 6-8

These article are designed to secure for all persons recognition and equality before the law and the protection of the law without discrimination.

Islam inculcates and upholds these values very clearly and firmly.

It lays down as a condition of faith that recourse must be had to the judicial process for the settlement of disputes. The judgment handed down must be accepted without demur and carried out fully (4:66). The Prophet himself was the first and the principal Judge at Medina and was commanded to judge justly between the people-Muslims, Jews and non Muslim Arabs, (42:16). 'Umar was also appointed a judge at Medina. The Prophet warned that the fact that a person had obtained a judgment in his favour did not confer on him a title to the subject-matter of the dispute, if in fact and in truth he was not entitled to it; for human judgment, his own or anyone else's, was liable to error.[55] He thus strengthened the process of administration of justice with a strong moral exhortation of accountability to God, which could not

[55] Bukhari IV, Sect.: Judgment's, Ch.: Admonition to Parties.

be evaded by taking shelter behind a judgment handed down by a fallible authority even so high as that of the Prophet.

Judges are admonished to carry out their duties with strict impartiality and justice. They are laid under the Divine injunction: "When you judge between the people, judge with justice. Surely, excellent is that with which Allah admonishes you! Allah is All-Hearing, All-Seeing" (4:59).

The course of justice is not to be sought to be corrupted through bribery (2:159) or the presentation of false evidence (25:73).

The hostility of a people should not incite a Muslim, or the Muslim Community or the Muslim State, to act unjustly or inequitably towards them. "O ye who believe, be steadfast in the cause of Allah, and bear witness in equity and let not a people's enmity toward you incite you to act otherwise than with justice. Be always just, that is closest to righteousness. Be ever mindful of your duty to Allah. Surely, Allah is aware of what you do" (5:9).

A more emphatic and comprehensive injunction is: "O ye who believe, be strict in observing justice, and bear your witness for the sake of Allah, even though it be against your own selves, or against parents or kindred.

Whether they be rich or poor, Allah is more regardful of them than you are. Therefore, guard yourselves against being led astray by low desires, so that you may be able to act equitably. If you conceal the truth or evade it, remember that Allah is well aware of what you do" (4:136).

'Umar, the second Khalifah, was cited as a defendant in a civil suit. When he came into Court to answer the claim preferred against him, the judge stood up as a mark of respect. 'Umar observed that he had come into Court not in his capacity as the Khalifah, but in his private capacity as a citizen, and that it was inconsistent with the judge's position for him to extend a courtesy to him which was not extended to every citizen appearing in Court. He held that the judge, by his action, had contravened his duty of impartiality toward the parties and was no longer fit to perform judicial functions.[56]

'Ali, the fourth Khalifah, also had occasion to appear in Court as a claimant against a Jew. In support of his claim, in addition to his own statement, he produced his eldest son Hasan as a witness in whose presence the obligation had been incurred by the defendant. The judge held that in view of the close relationship between

[56] Kanz-el-Ummal III, p. 174; Shibli Nu'mani, Al-Farooq II, p. 166.

the plaintiff and the witness, the testimony of the witness was not admissible and he dismissed the claim. The defendant was so impressed that immediately upon emerging from the court room he acknowledged the claim and discharged it.[57]

Articles 9-11

These articles are designed to provide safeguards against the arbitrary exercise of executive or administrative authority and in respect of the due administration of justice where a criminal charge is involved and a penalty might be incurred. They are part of the system of checks and balances which experience through the centuries has shown to be desirable as a curb upon the tendency towards despotism. The spirit underlying them has been discussed under Articles 6-8, and it need only be added that whatever safeguards experience might demonstrate to be needful for carrying that spirit into effect should be acceptable. As seen already, Islam not only seeks to uphold the basic values through legislative safeguards, but strives constantly to ensure their observance in every sphere by

[57] Rahmatullah Subhani, Makhzan-i-Akhlaq, p. 229.

emphasizing the moral responsibility of all concerned- the individual, society, and the State.

Article 12

This article falls in the same broad category as Articles 9-11, only it touches upon matters that concern each individual more intimately, being more personal in their nature. Islam goes further than any other system in safeguarding these, not only vis-a-vis the State, but also vis-a-vis other citizens.

"O ye who believe, enter not houses other than your own until you have asked leave and saluted the inmates thereof; that is better for you that you may be heedful. If you find no one therein, do not enter them till you are given permission. If it be said to you, 'Go back'. then go back, that is purer for you. Allah knows well what you do. But it is no offence on your part to enter uninhabited houses wherein are your goods. Allah knows that which you disclose and that which you conceal" (24:28-30).

Muslim jurisprudence recognizes and gives effect through legal procedures, to what is known as the easement of privacy. After a prescribed period, premises used for residence acquire the right of enjoyment of undisturbed privacy against any structure proposed to be constructed thereafter which would interfere seriously with that enjoyment.

Certain climatic and cultural considerations come into play in connection with this easement. But even in temperate regions, under the pressure of growing urban communities, privacy in western countries also is beginning to be unduly interfered with, and some relief may have to be sought by making due allowance for that very legitimate need in building and housing regulations.

Another doctrine of Muslim jurisprudence tends in the same direction, that is to say towards stressing and safeguarding some of the values set out in this article.

Sales of urban residential property are, under Islamic law, subject to the right of pre-emption. Briefly, this may be explained as the right of an owner of contiguous property, or of property enjoying an easement against or being subject to an easement in favour of property which is proposed to be sold, to purchase it, if he so wishes, in preference to another not possessing an equal or superior right of purchase. If a sale takes place in contravention of this right, the right may be enforced through judicial process. The purchaser then has to give way to the pre-emptor, who is entitled to be substituted in place of the purchaser on payment to him of the price actually paid by him for the premises.

Great stress is laid in Islam on kindness to and benevolence towards a neighbour. "Worship Allah and associate naught with Him, and behave benevolently towards parents, kindred, orphans and the needy, and the neighbour that is a kinsman and the neighbour that is a stranger, and the companion by your side and the wayfarer, and those whom your right hands possess. Surely, Allah loves not the proud and the boastful, who are niggardly and enjoin people to be niggardly and conceal that which Allah has bestowed upon them of His bounty" (4:37-38).

The Prophet laid repeated stress on the duty owed to a neighbour. He said on one occasion, "So often and so much has God impressed upon me the duty owed to a neighbour that I began to think that a neighbour might perhaps be named an heir".[58]

In his Farewell Address he declared, "Your lives, your properties and your honour are declared sacred as the sanctity attaching to this day (the day of Pilgrimage) and this month and this spot".[59]

[58] Bukhari IV, Sect.:Good Behaviour, Ch.:Benevolence towards Neighbours.

[59] Hanbal V, p. 411.

Such is the concern of Islam for the individual and what he owes to his fellow men, particularly those with whom he has to be in close contact. It is thus clear that the objectives of Article 12 are fully supported and subscribed to by Islam.

Articles 13-15

These articles relate to nationality, freedom of movement and residence, and asylum.

From the standpoint of Islam the scope and effect of these articles, by virtue of the underlying implications, are restrictive of the freedom of the individual rather than enlarging and protective.

For instance, the first paragraph of Article 13, though expressed in wide and general terms, is subject to the implied condition that the person claiming the right must either be a national of the State within the borders of which he wishes freely to move and reside, or must have obtained admission to its territory in compliance with its laws and regulations pertaining to such admission.

The second paragraph spells out the right to leave a country, but, with the exception of a person's own country, does not concern itself with the right of entry into a country.

Thus the operation of the article is circumscribed by the immigration laws of different States and their regulations concerning passports, visas, and entry and exit permits. In today's conditions that is perhaps unavoidable but it is none-the-less regrettable. The world seems at the moment to be held firmly to the pattern of a conglomeration of national States, with all the divisive, disruptive, disturbing and dangerous policies, tendencies and consequences thereby generated and maintained in a state of intensive ferment.

The dangers and threats inherent in this pattern are being realized and appraised more and more widely, and movements towards closer relations, regional and continental, are developing. In the meantime one must, one supposes, reconcile oneself to the prevailing pattern and make the best of it.

The primary function of religion is to create and strengthen faith in a Beneficent Creator and in the hierarchy of values within the purview of religion, where the moral and the spiritual must take precedence over the rest, though Islam seeks to bring about beneficent adjustment in all spheres of life.

Islam, while taking note of the diversity of tongues and colours and describing them as Signs from which those who possess knowledge may draw lessons (30:23), does not treat this or any other diversity as creating a division among mankind. It addresses itself to the whole of mankind and the form of address is "O mankind" or "O people", the Arabic expression in both cases being the same i.e. *annas*. 'Specific commandments and directions are addressed to those who have pledged allegiance to Islam. They are addressed as "O ye who believe". The attitude of a Muslim is, therefore, that of a true universalist, or vis-a-vis today's political pattern, that of an internationalist, rather than that of a narrow nationalist. It is realized, however, that progress towards Internationaism and an International Community is in today's conditions, which are a legacy of the immediate past, possible only from the starting-point of national sovereignty and independence. A people must be in possession and enjoyment of national independence and sovereignty before, even from the juridical point of view, it can pool any portion thereof for common purposes, whether regional or International.

It is against this background that we may attempt a useful and profitable appraisal and appreciation of these articles of the Declaration.

Islam does not contemplate any restriction on freedom of movement and residence, whether within a

State or beyond its borders. Indeed the Quran accounts facilities for easy and secure travel as a bounty of Allah, neglect or nonappreciation of which might attract its own penalty. Of the people of Saba it says: "We placed, between them and the towns that We had blessed, other towns that were prominently visible, and We fixed easy stages between them: Travel between them night and day in security. But they said: Our Lord, make the stages of our journeys longer. Thus they wronged themselves" (34:19-20).

One of the major obligations ordained by Islam, for those who can afford to discharge it is the Pilgrimage to Mecca, which was first instituted by Abraham. "We assigned to Abraham the site of the House, and said: Associate not anything with Me, and keep My House pure for those who perform the circuits and those who stand up and those who bow down and fall prostrate in Prayer, and proclaim unto mankind the Pilgrimage. They will come to thee on foot and on every lean camel, travelling by every distant track·' (22:27-28). This implies the right of free movement across continents and oceans. In the succeeding verses and elsewhere in the Quran are spelt out the benefits, spiritual as well as material, that flow from the Pilgrimage.

Travel sharpens understanding and promotes

appreciation of moral and spiritual values, through observation and the acquisition of knowledge and information. "How many a city have We destroyed, because it was given to wrongdoing, so that it is fallen down on its roofs; and how many a deserted well and lofty castle! Have they not travelled in the earth that they may have hearts wherewith to understand, or ears wherewith to hear? Verily, it is not the eyes that are blind, but the hearts which are in the breasts that are blind" (22:46-47).

Valuable lessons could be drawn from the contemplation of the histories of peoples who have passed away. "Surely, there have been many dispensations before you; so travel through the earth and see how evil was the end of those who treated God's Messengers as liars" (3:138).

Pondering over evidences of the process of creation would facilitate faith in the assurance of the spiritual revival of a people and the life after death. "See they not how Allah originates creation, then repeats it? That surely is easy for Allah. Say: Travel in the earth, and observe how He originated the creation. Then will Allah provide the later creation. Surely Allah has power over all things" (29:20-21).

Attention is invited through travel to the rise and fall

of peoples, some of them stronger, more powerful and more advanced than those who succeeded them, and the causes thereof, so that those reminded may take heed and mend their ways in time. "They know only the outer aspect of the life of this world, and of the Hereafter they are utterly unmindful. Do they not reflect in their own minds? Allah has not created the heavens and the earth and all that is between the two but in accordance with the requirements of wisdom and for a fixed term. But many among men believe not in the meeting with their Lord. Have they not travelled in the earth that they might see how evil was the end of those that were before them? They were stronger than these in power, and they cultivated the soil and populated the land more and better than these have done. Their Messengers came to them with manifest signs; Allah would not wrong them but they wronged their own souls. Then evil was the end of those who did evil, because they rejected the Signs of Allah and mocked at them" (30:8-11).

Travel thus widens horizons, increases knowledge, promotes understanding, stimulates intellect and deepens appreciation of Divine purposes. It fosters moral and spiritual values which are the primary concern of religion.

"He shows you His Signs; which then of the Signs of

Allah will you deny?

"Have they not travelled in the earth that they might observe the end of those who were before them? They were more numerous than these, and mightier in power and in the traces that they left behind them in the earth. But all that they earned was of no avail to them.

"When their Messengers came to them with manifest Signs they exulted in the knowledge which they possessed, but that at which they mocked encompassed them" (40:82-83).

The purposes of travel and movement which the Quran stresses are wider and more comprehensive than those that underlie Article 13; those that are aimed at by the article are included among those emphasized by the Quran. While, however, the Quran proceeds on the assumption that it is open to all God's creatures to move freely in the earth and to sojourn therein at choice, the article confines and limits the right to be exercised "within the borders of each State".

It is worthy of note that prior to 1914 the right to freedom of movement was much wider and less restricted than it is today. It is an irony that so long as the means of travel were restricted, travel itself was freer; when the means were improved and travel became faster, man's freedom to avail himself of these facilities was subjected to arbitrary, vexatious and irritating restrictions. In this respect there has been visible retrogression, temporarily justifiable, and perhaps even necessary, particularly during periods of war, but which is tending to become a permanent and normal restraint upon free human intercourse. International travel is becoming more and more a privilege rather than a freedom.

Were international travel free and unrestricted the right to seek and enjoy asylum (Article 14) would lose the greater part of its significance. Subject to the provisions of Treaties regulating Extradition, everyone could go where he liked without let or hindrance.

Islam strongly supports the right to seek and enjoy asylum from persecution. All forms of persecution are affronts to human dignity, but from the point of view of religion the worst is persecution in respect of matters of faith and conscience.

In the early years, Islam and the Muslims were subjected to bitter and cruel persecution by the Quraish in Mecca. As life began to be made insupportable for them in Mecca the Prophet counselled some of them to leave Mecca and to seek asylum across the Red Sea in Ethiopia, where they might find conditions more endurable under the rule of the Christian Emperor. A small party, under the leadership of a cousin of the

Prophet, went across, but were followed by a delegation of the Quraish, who demanded that the fugitives be delivered over to them. The Emperor heard both sides and rejected the demands of the Meccans, assuring the Muslims that they could dwell in the land without fear of molestation.[60]

Later, as persecution continued to mount in Mecca and a number of the people of Medina had accepted Islam and had expressed their willingness to receive and afford assistance to their harassed and persecuted brethren of Mecca, the Prophet directed that those who could do so should migrate to Medina.[61] When almost all who were free to do so had migrated to Medina, he himself received the Divine command to leave Mecca and to proceed to Medina. He performed the journey at great hazard, in the company of Abu Bakr, one of his earliest and most devoted followers.[62]

Since their foremost obligation, the upholding of moral and spiritual values as a community, had been made impossible for them in Mecca, emigration from

60 Sirat lbn Hisham I, Ch.:Migration to Ethiopia.

61 Bukhari II, Sect.:Beginning of Creation, Ch.:Migration of the Holy Prophet and His Companions to Medina.

62 Ibid.

Mecca was made obligatory upon them, "except in the case of such weak ones among men, women and children as are incapable of adopting any plan or of finding any way" (4:99). For the strong and able-bodied, who were not prevented by *force majeure* from departing and who chose to stay on, any default in the discharge of their obligations would not be excusable on the plea that they were in too weak a position to uphold the values of their faith in the midst of so much hostility and such bitter persecution. "Verily, from those whom the angels cause to die while they are wronging their own souls they will enquire: What were you after? They will reply: We were treated as weak in the land. The angels will retort: Was not Allah's earth vast enough for you to emigrate therein?" (4:98).

So that in the situation in which the Muslims found themselves in Mecca, the seeking of asylum was not merely a device to which they could have recourse for the purpose of obtaining relief from persecution, it became a duty and an obligation. In a similar situation anywhere, at any time, the duty and the obligation would be revived, so that moral and spiritual values should have the opportunity of flourishing under conditions of reasonable freedom and should not be placed in peril of being suppressed by hostility and persecution. For those who are forced to leave hearth and home so that they may be able to uphold their consciences and do their duty to their Maker in utter sincerity, there is the promise of Divine support and succour.

"Whoso emigrates for the sake of Allah will find in the earth an abundant place of refuge and plentifulness; and whoso goes forth from his home, emigrating in the cause of Allah and His Messenger, and death overtakes him, his reward lies with Allah, and Allah is Most Forgiving, Merciful" (4:101).

Those who subordinate all other considerations to the cause of righteousness and are steadfast, putting their trust in their Lord, will find a sure support in Him, both here and Hereafter. "Those who have migrated from their homes for the sake of Allah after they had been wronged We will surely provide them with a goodly refuge in this world, and truly the reward of the Hereafter is greater if they but knew-those who are steadfast and put their trust in their Lord" (16:42-43).

"Surely, thy Lord-to those who migrated from their homes after they had been persecuted and then put forth every effort in support of righteousness and remained steadfast-aye, surely, after that thy Lord is Most Forgiving, Merciful" (16:111).

Those who flee from persecution may not survive

their search for a place of refuge; even so, if their effort was in the cause of righteousness it shall not have been in vain. "Those who migrate from their homes for the sake of Allah, and are then slain or die, Allah will surely provide for them a goodly provision. Surely Allah is the Best Provider. He will surely cause them to enter a haven with which they will be well pleased. Allah is indeed AllKnowing, Forbearing" (22:59-60).

To welcome those who have left their homes for the sake of righteousness is highly meritorious and opens the way to prosperity. "Those who had established their homes in this city before them and had accepted faith, love those who come to them for refuge, and find not in their breasts any desire for that which is bestowed upon the newcomers, but prefer them to their own selves even though they themselves are poor. Whoso is rid of the covetousness of his own soul-it is these who will prosper" (59:10).

So much for asylum against persecution of conscience when men may be forced to leave their homes and whatever they hold dear-lands, properties, occupations, relations, associations and a whole set of social and cultural values-in the effort to preserve that which they hold above everything else, namely, their duty to their Maker. But there may be other cases in which asylum can be legitimately requested and granted. Islam recognizes the need of and makes provision for asylum even during the progress of hostilities.

"If anyone of the (warring) idolaters ask thee for asylum, grant him asylum so that he may hear the Word of Allah; then convey him to his place of security. That is because they are a people who lack knowledge" (9:6).

The doctrine of nationality is a result of the division of mankind into political groups on the basis mainly of geographical boundaries. Social, cultural, economic, lingguistic and even religious considerations may intrude themselves into the concept, but the major element is furnished by territorial limits. So long as the current political patterns and divisions are maintained, considerable value and importance must continue to be attached to nationality and the right to a nationality must be recognized and safeguarded. Many factors may make it desirable for an individual, or for a group of individuals, whether members of the same family or not, to give up one nationality and acquire another in its place. The provisions of Article 15, therefore, are in today's conditions almost axiomatic. A person without a nationality, or a stateless person, would find himself seriously handicapped and circumscribed. Yet nationality, the laws regulating nationality and the privileges, duties and obligations pertaining to nationality are not in all cases and in all circumstances an unmitigated blessing. Trends are already perceptible towards the recognition of a bond of human fellowship transcending nationality. In many respects the bond of nationality is beginning to be felt as too restrictive and confining, and some of the demands that it makes upon an individual as a constraint upon the free development of personality.

Islam aims at universality and addresses itself to the whole of mankind as constituting one fellowship. It recognizes only two broad divisions within that fellowship, based not upon region, country, sex, race, colour, language or the like, but upon moral standards and the lack of them, beneficence and non-beneficence, righteous conduct and wrong-doing. Apart from legal sanctions designed to restrain such wrongs as are deemed offences or crimes, its sanctions are also moral and spiritual. Its purpose is to save and not to destroy, to join together and not to put asunder.

The Quran opens with the words: "All praise belongs to Allah, Lord of all the worlds, the Gracious, the Merciful, Master of the Day of Judgment" (1:2-4), and it closes with the prayer: Say: I seek refuge with the Lord of mankind, the King of mankind, the God of mankind, from the evil of the sneaking whisperer, who whispers into the hearts of men" (114:2-6).

Its usual form of address for purposes of exhortation is: "O mankind", while commandments, injunctions and directions are addressed to those who profess allegiance to it as: "O ye who believe".

The expressions "*ummah*" and "*qaum*", which in the present age are employed as equivalents of "nations", are used in the Quran as meaning simply "people". Other expressions are used for tribes, sub-tribes, groups and sections, but there is no expression employed to connote or denote "nation" or "nationality" in the sense in which these terms are used in Article 15 of the Declaration.

Article 16

This article deals with the right to marry, equal rights of the parties to a marriage, consent to marriage and the protection of the family.

It thus touches upon some aspects of what is known in certain legal systems as Personal Law or the Law of Personal Relationships. It must be construed liberally and not literally; for literal construction of, for instance, the first paragraph of the article would lead to results some of which would border on absurdity while others would be abhorrent as offending against universally accepted norms and standards of decency.

The only limitations upon the right to marry recognized by the article are that the parties should be of full age and should give their full and free consent to the marriage. Yet it is obvious that the article is not intended to be construed as authorizing marriage between father and daughter, mother and son, brother and sister, though there is nothing in the language of the article to suggest that such unions would be repugnant either to its letter or to its spirit. It might be urged that the article could not have been intended to authorize unions within the prohibited degrees. Even if that were to be accepted as the obvious intention and meaning of the article, how are prohibited degrees to be determined? The article says the right to marry shall be enjoyed without any limitation due to religion, while the notion of prohibited degrees, in its essence and its origin, has its root in religion. Besides, once one gets away from the first-degree relationships mentioned above, prohibited degrees vary very widely in different religious systems, and all of them constitute limitations on marriage "due to religion". Would such limitations prescribed by one religious system be accorded validity under the article and those prescribed by another be rejected? This aspect could be amply illustrated by comparison of specific prohibitions in different systems and could be expatiated upon, but that is not necessary for our immediate purpose.

Another complication is added by the conflict that has developed between the Canon Law and the Civil Law under some systems.

It must be realized, therefore, that in a matter so personal and so intimate and so much intertwined with religion it would be too broad a proposition to be universally acceptable that subject to the parties being of full age and consenting fully and freely to the union, they must be accorded the right to marry without any limitation due to religion.

The second sentence of the first paragraph of the article can also lead to difficulties in implementation, if strictly construed. For instance, at the dissolution of a marriage, where there are children of the marriage, questions of guardianship and custody might be involved, in respect of which it might be difficult to observe equality between the conflicting claims of the mother and the father. As we shall see, Islamic Law seeks to resolve these and other questions arising at the dissolution of a marriage in a spirit of equity between the parties, with due regard to the welfare of the children affected and the competing claims of natural affection.

The dissolution of marriage and a host of other matters relating to marriage and resulting therefrom must under many systems continue to be governed by values based upon religion, and it would be unrealistic to try to by-pass them. Faith in a religion means that a believer commits himself or herself to bring his or her life into conformity with the values inculcated by that religion. Should the Declaration be in conflict with any of those values, the Declaration must give way, and not that in which a person truly believes. The fundamental values of religion must, prevail against all other values and considerations, else religion would cease to have meaning and reality and would serve merely as a cloak for hypocrisy.

Islam regards the married life as the normal state and does not look with favour upon celibacy or monasticism (27:28). The Prophet said: "Married life is our way; whoever turns away from our way is not of us",[63] and declared: "There is no monasticism in Islam".[64]

The Islamic concept of marriage is a union for the

[63] Muslim I, Sect.:Marriage, Ch.:Desirability of Marriage etc.

[64] Habal VI, p. 226.

purpose of promoting righteousness and seeking the fulfilment of the purpose of life both here and Hereafter.

On the occasion of the announcement of a marriage (public announcement being one of the requisites of a valid marriage) the Prophet always recited these verses of the Quran:

"O ye people, be mindful of your duty to your Lord, Who created you from a single soul and created therefrom its mate, and from them twain multiplied many men and women. Be mindful of your duty to Allah, in Whose name you appeal to one another, and be mindful of the ties of kinship. Verily, Allah watches over you" (4:2).

"O ye who believe, be mindful of your duty to Allah and say the straight-forward word; thereby will He make your conduct beneficent and forgive you your defaults Whoso obeys Allah and His Messenger, shall surely attain a mighty success" (33:71-72).

"O ye who believe, be mindful of your duty to Allah, and let every soul look to what it sends forth for the morrow. Be mindful of your duty to Allah; verily Allah is Well-Aware of what you do" (59:19).

The Prophet warned that the purpose of marriage has the best chance of being achieved if the choice of a spouse is determined primarily by moral and spiritual considerations and not by looks, family or wealth.[65]

Marriage should, through the constant experience of mutual love and tenderness between the spouses, be a source of fulfilment and peace of mind. "One of His Signs is that He has created spouses for you from among yourselves that you may find peace of mind in them, and He has put love and tenderness between you. In that surely are Signs for a people who reflect" (30:32).

The general exhortation is added: "Consort with them in kindness: for even if you dislike them, it may be that you dislike something wherein Allah has placed much good" (4:20).

The Prophet said: "The best of you is he who behaves best towards the members of his family".[66]

Thus repeated emphasis is laid on seeking the will and pleasure of Allah in all things and putting that before personal inclination and preferences.

Despite all this, allowance is made for the frailty and changeableness of human nature. Thus it has not been sought, in Islam, to convert marriage into an indissoluble sacrament. It is in its legal aspect a civil contract in which the rights and obligations of the parties are clearly

---

65 Muslim I, Sect.:Giving Suck to Children.

66 Ibn Maja II, Ch.:Marriage, Good Behaviour towards Women.

defined, but everything is made subject to seeking the pleasure of God and the fulfilment of one's duty to Him. The relationship is intended to be permanent, but dissolution is permissible under certain conditions and subject to safeguards. Concerning dissolution of marriage by divorce the Prophet has said: "Of all things permitted to you the most obnoxious in the sight of Allah is divorce".[67]

Article 16 of the Declaration declares that men and women are entitled to equal rights as to marriage, during marriage, and at its dissolution.

The status of men and women in marriage within any particular social system is determined largely by the position assigned to men and women vis-a-vis one another in that system. So far as a system is based upon and derives its values from religion, the crucial factor in this regard would be the relative positions assigned to the sexes in respect of the possibility of attainment of the spiritual ideals proclaimed by that religion.

Islam makes no distinction whatever between the sexes in that respect.

"The believers, men and women, are friends one of another. They enjoin good and forbid evil and observe

[67] Abu Daud II, Sect.:Divorce, Ch.:Divorce is obnoxious.

Prayer and pay the *Zakat* and obey Allah and His Messenger. It is these on whom Allah will have mercy. Surely, Allah is Mighty, Wise.

"Allah has promised to believers, men and women, gardens beneath which streams flow, wherein they will abide, and delightful dwelling-places in gardens of Eternity. But the pleasure of Allah is the greatest of all bounties. That is the supreme triumph" (9:71-72).

Thus neither in respect of opportunities and capacity for beneficent action, nor in respect of ultimate attainment is there any differentiation between the sexes.

More specially is it proclaimed: "Surely, men who submit themselves to God and women who submit themselves to Him, and believing men and believing women, and obedient men and obedient women, and truthful men and truthful women, and steadfast men and steadfast women, and men who humble themselves before God and women who humble themselves before Him, and men who give alms and women who give alms, and men who fast and women who fast, and men who guard their chastity and women who guarrd their chastity, and men who remember Allah much and women who remember Him much-Allah has prepared for all of them forgiveness and a great reward" (33:36).

Men and women are equally entitled to protection against calumny and persecution. "Those who malign believing men and believing women for what they have not earned shall bear the guilt of calumny and a manifest sin" (33:59), and "Those who persecute the believing men and the believing women and then repent not, for them is surely the chastisement of the Fire, and for them is the punishment of burning" (85:11).

The mercy and forgiveness of Allah are extended equally to men and women: "Allah turns in mercy to believing men and believing women, and Allah is Most Forgiving, Merciful" (33:74).

The Prophet is exhorted to pray for both men and women: "Know, therefore, that there is no god other than Allah, and ask forgiveness for thy frailties, and for the believing men and the believing women. Allah knows the place wherein you move about and the place wherein you abide" (47:20).

In the Hereafter both men and women will be accorded the light of God's pleasure: "Think of the day when thou wilt see the believing men and the believing women, their light running before them and on their right hands, and it will be said of them, 'Glad tidings for you this day! Gardens through which streams flow, wherein you will abide. That is the supreme triumph'"

(57:13), and their prayer will be: "Our Lord, perfect unto us our light and remove our shortcomings, surely Thou hast power over all things" (66:9).

As models for those who believe, Allah has set forth the example of two women-the wife of Pharaoh, who besought Allah for deliverance from Pharoah and all his works, and Mary, mother of Jesus. who "fulfilled in her person the words of her Lord and His Books and was one of the obedient" (66:12-13).

Yet Islam takes note of the diversity of roles and functions assigned to men and women and makes due provision for them.

God, in His Providence and Wisdom, has equipped men and women appropriately for the due fulfilment and discharge of the roles and functions which belong to each. In structure man is stronger and of rougher texture than woman, who is more delicate and of greater sensibility. Were that not so there would be little attraction between the two, and the foundation for the "love and tenderness" between them (30:22) would be lacking.

The element of mutual attraction and co-operation, essential for the continuation of the species and for the promotion of social values, is expressed in the terms: "They (your spouses) are raiment for you and you are raiment for them" (2:188). Raiment serves many purposes. It is a covering for such parts of the body as should not be exposed to view and is also a source of elegance and delight (7:27). It affords protection and comfort against weather and climate and against harmful and injurious substances. Of all man's possessions it stands in the closest and most intimate relationship to him. Husband and wife are all this to each other, only very much more so. For while man's relationship with articles of dress is purely physical, the relationship between husband and wife is a union which involves their total personalities in all their aspects. One aspect of this relationship is that in many respects it is complementary, which emphasizes and enhances its character and value, but also necessitates a certain degree of discrimination, beneficial and not prejudicial, both in respect of its object and its operation.

The concept of equality must be viewed and appraised against the background and character of the relationship which marriage is designed to establish between the spouses. Woman is in many respects more vulnerable than man and therefore, is in greater need of protection and security. Islam takes account of this and makes due provision for it where needed. For instance, while men and women are both protected against calumny and persecution (33:59), one particular species of calumny against a woman, namely, an imputation against her chastity, is condemned in much harsher terms and is made subject to a severer penalty. It is included among those few crimes for which the Quran itself specifies the punishment. "Verily those who make false accusations against chaste, unwary, believing women are cursed in this world and the Hereafter, and for them is a grievous chastisement, on the day when their tongues and their hands and their feet shall bear witness against them as to what they used to do. On that day will Allah mete out to them their just due, and they will know that Allah alone is the Manifest Truth" (24:24-26). "Those who make accusations against chaste women and bring not four witnesses in support thereof-flog them with eighty stripes, and never admit their evidence thereafter; it is they that are the transgressors, except those who repent thereafter and make amends, for truly Allah is Most Forgiving, Merciful" (24:5-6).

Islam recognizes that "the family is the natural and fundamental group unit of society" (Art. 16-3) and not only accords it the fullest protection but also shows how that protection can be made effective. It does not accept or endorse the attitude, more and more current in certain sections of society, that the sanctity of the marriage covenant, which lies at the root of all family relationships and supports, sustains and nourishes them, may be freely exposed to every kind of pre-marital and post-marital hazard and yet survive unblemished and unscathed.

In the final analysis everything hinges on the hierarchy of values; that is to say, in the event of competition or conflict, which must have preference and which must give way. A society that seeks to give concurrent effect to conflicting values is already straining at the seams of its fabric and will burst them sooner or later. Measured in terms of the span of individual human lives, the process might appear to be slow, it might be well-nigh imperceptible; viewed against the background of history its march and progress cannot fail to be clearly discerned. In its final stages it rushes along unrestrained and unchecked, for then no effort and no force can avail to arrest it. The crash becomes inevitable.

Promiscuity and family values are utterly incompatible; they cannot for long subsist together. If the one is not sternly suppressed, the other will disintegrate. There is no other choice. To think otherwise is to practice outrageous deception upon oneself and upon society. In this, as in the case of other evils, Islam, in conformity with its function as a religion, seeks to stem the mischief at the very source.

Where does it originate? In this particular case it starts when the eye goes aroving. Other senses then come in, eagerly or with feigned reluctance, each helping and nudging the others along: touch, smell, hearing, voice, all play their part, and the co-ordinated, organized pursuit of the objective has begun. The process is conscious and calculated, whatever pretence may be feined for the benefit of third parties. "Nay, man is a witness over his self, even though he puts forward his excuses" (75:15-16). In the early stages he may reassure himself that he has given no one any cause to entertain the least suspicion, but there is One Who knows the treachery of the eyes and what the breasts conceal" (40:20).

What is the remedy? First, strict control of the senses and a constant watch over them lest any of them should stray from the path of righteousness and beneficence; for each one of them is responsible and will be called to account. "Pursue not that of which thou hast not knowledge. Verily, the ear and the eye and the heart-everyone of them will be called to account" (37:17). Secondly, reduction to the minimum practicable of the display of feminine charm and beauty which might attract and incite, first, curiosity, then the urge to know, and finally the desire for intimacy. For certain societies the restraint thus required of both men and women might in today's conditions be considered revolutionary. It would not have been so regarded up to the First World War, though even then it would have entailed considerable adjustments in social intercourse and deportment. Today the situation is rapidly passing beyond remedy.

The Quran first sets out what are described as "the limits prescribed by Allah". For instance, "These are the limits prescribed by Allah, so transgress them not; and whoso transgresses the limits prescribed by Allah, it is they that are the wrongdoers" (2:230). It then enjoins alertness in watching the limits set by Allah. "Rejoice then, in your bargain that you have made with Him; and that it is which is the supreme triumph. These are the ones who tum to God in repentence, who worship Him, who praise Him, who go out in the land serving Him, who bow down to Him, who prostrate themselves in Prayer, who enjoin equity and forbid iniquity, and who watch the limits set by Allah. Give thou glad tidings to those who have faith" (9:11-12).

It then goes on to admonish that the surest way of observing the limits set by Allah is to keep well away from them, "to go not nigh unto them". "These are the limits set by Allah, so go not nigh unto them. Thus does Allah make His commandments clear to people that they may become secure against evil" (2:188). What has been made clear in this context is that "to become secure against evil" one must not proceed to the point where one is directly confronted by the evil, but one must stop short even of the approaches to it. When it beckons from afar one must resist the temptation to dally with it; one must aschew even the innocent-seeming preliminaries to it; one must not seek to deceive oneself and must realize whither they would lead.

We can now appreciate the wisdom of the injunction, "Come not nigh unto adultery, surely it is a foul act and an evil way" (17:33). This is not only an injunction against adultery, it bars all appoaches to it, beginning with stolen glances and fugitive smiles and culminating in the foul consummation by way of innuendo, hand-clasp, caress and embrace.

The injunction is not confined to the extreme case of adultery; it applies to every kind of evil, overt or covert. "Approach not indecencies, whether open or secret" (6:152). That is the only way to security against all manner of evil, maugre vehement protestations of innocence of design and purity of intention. "Whether you conceal what you say or proclaim it, He knows well what is in your breasts. Would He not know, Who has created you? Aye, He is the Knower of all subtleties, the All-Aware" (67:14-15). "He knows the treachery of the eyes and what the breasts conceal" (40:20).

The specific injunctions designed to secure marriage and the family against undue hazard are: "Say, O Prophet, to the believing men that they restrain their eyes and watch over their senses. Surely, Allah is well aware of what they do. And say to the believing women that they restrain their eyes and watch over their senses and disclose not their charm except that which is perforce apparent thereof, and that they drape their head-coverings over their bosoms and that they disclose not their charm except to their husbands", or to other relations within the prohibited degrees, or their female attendants or their male attendants of such advanced age as to be beyond the reach of temptation, or children of tender age not yet conscious of difference of sex; "and that they strike not their feet together in walking so as to disclose their hidden ornaments. And turn ye to Allah all together. O believers, that you may prosper" (24:31-32).

Here, within a brief compass, is a whole code of social conduct and deportment which, if sincerely and strictly followed, would ensure the sanctity of the marriage covenant and the stability of the family.

The restraints imposed are, up to a point identical in the case of men and women; an additional safeguard, in the interest of both men and women, is added which has to be observed by women, as they are the ones who have been invested with the additional quality that charms and subdues. They alone can be the guardians of it in the context under consideration.

But there are many other factors which operate within the sphere of marital relationship which entitle the fairer and the frailer sex to consideration and protecting care on the part of the stronger sex. Some of these stem from their respective functions and spheres of activity. In anticipation of motherhood and after achievement of that sacred dignity, woman is entitled to certain privileges, exemptions, and a degree of additional care which it is the duty, and should be the pride, of the husband to provide and make available.

Also, in normal circumstances, the husband's sphere of activity is the office, the workshop, the factory, the field, the legislature, and in times of peril, the front line. The greater part of the wife's solicitude, care and attention is claimed by the home and children. This position has, in recent times, been placed in unbalance, with little advantage and considerable damage to all beneficent values. Some women have been inclined to put a career above home and the care, upbringing and training of children, others have been compelled to make that choice under economic pressure or necessity. Islam disapproves of the first and seeks to relieve and remedy the second.

It assigns to parents and especially to the mother a position of great dignity and honour. "Thy Lord has decreed that you worship none but Him, and conduct yourselves benevolently towards parents. If one of them or both of them attain old age with thee, address not to them any word expressive of impatience or annoyance, nor reproach them, and speak kindly to them. Lower to them the wing of humility out of tenderness and pray: "My Lord, have mercy on them even as they nourished me when I was little" (17:24-25).

"We have enjoined on man to conduct himself benevolently towards his parents. His mother bears him in travail and brings him forth in travail, and the bearing of him and his weaning takes thirty months, till when he attains his full maturity and reaches the age of forty years, he prays: My Lord, grant me that I may be grateful for Thy favour which Thou hast bestowed upon me and upon my parents, and that I may act righteously so as to please Thee, and make also my issue righteous. I do turn to Thee; and truly, I am of those who submit to Thee. Those are they of whom We accept the best of what they do and overlook their ill deeds. They shall be among the inmates of the Garden, in fulfilment of the true promise which was made to them" (46:16-17).

The Prophet said: "Paradise lies under the feet of your mothers".[68] When someone asked him which of his relations was most deserving of his care and attention, he replied, "Thy mother". "And after her?" enquired the questioner. "Thy father", said the Prophet.[69]

A man came to him and asked permission to go to the front. "Are thy parents alive?" enquired the Prophet. On receiving an affirmative reply, the Prophet said: "Occupy thyself with looking after them, that will be the equivalent of thy military service".[70]

On one occasion he observed: "Most unfortunate is the person whose parents are aged and who fails to win Paradise through taking good care of them".[71]

To a mother her child is blood of her blood and life

---

[68] As-Sayuti.

[69] Bukhari II, Sect.:Good Behaviour, Ch.:Who is most deserving of kindly treatment.

[70] Bukhari II, Sect.:Jehad, etc., Ch.:Permission of parents for Jehad.

[71] Muslim II, Sect.:Virtue, etc., Ch.:Priority of care of Parents, etc.

of her life. The chords, manifold and mysterious, that bind the two together, though invisible, are indissoluble and continue to exercise their irresistible pull not only throughout their joint lives but also from beyond the grave, during the temporary separation of one from the other which must be endured in the course of nature. A mother who, except in cases of imperative and inescapable necessity (and a call of pleasure, diversion, amusement or social obligation could scarcely be represented as falling under that category) transfers the supreme joy and privilege of looking after her child to a baby-sitter or other substitute, bearing a more sophisticated title, to that degree abdicates a sacred and holy office.

As regards economic necessity, the obligation of making due provision for mother and child rests under the Islamic economic system, upon the father and no part of it is to be borne by the mother. Where the father is not able to discharge the obligation, it must be assumed and discharged by the State. If the mother has means of her own she may make such contribution as she pleases, but is not under any obligatfon to do so.

Men and women are entitled to the share of their incomes and earnings which, under the law may be assigned to individual appropriation. "Covet not that whereby Allah has made some of you excel others. Men shall have a share of that which they have earned, and women a share of that which they have earned. Ask Allah of His bounty. Surely, Allah has perfect knowledge of all things" (4:33).

But the obligation to provide security and protection and to make provision for the needs of the family lies on the husband. In a partnership involving mutual obligations, the partner who must carry the heavier responsibility must also have a larger say in the final determination of affairs that attract that responsibility. The husband or father, because of his superior physical strength and more robust capacities and qualities, must be responsible for security and protection. He must be the guardian. On account of his economic and financial responsibility he should have control over expenditure. "Men are guardians over women because Allah has made some of them excel others and because of that which they have to spend of their wealth" (4:135). Should differences arise and become serious and persist and a breach be threatened, recourse should be had to a process of conciliation. "If you fear a breach between them, then appoint an arbiter from his people and an arbiter from her people. If they desire reconciliation, Allah will effect it between them. Surely Allah is All-

Knowing, All-Aware" (4:36).

To enable the husband to meet his financial obligations in connection with and resulting from the marriage-e.g. a settlement on the wife is obligatory in every case (4:5) and the provision for the maintenance of the family-the share of a male in inheritance is double that of a female in the same degree of relationship to the propositus, except in the case of a father and mother, who in most cases have an equal share (4:12).

A part of the protection extended to a woman is that in addition to her own consent to marriage the consent of her guardian is also requisite. This is designed to safeguard her against the hazards attendant upon an unwise choice due to ignorance or lack of, adequate knowledge of the character, habits, disposition, family or other circumstances of the prospective bridegroom. If she feels that her guardian is withholding his consent unreasonably or capriciously, she can apply to the Qazi (Judge) who, if satisfied, can overrule the guardian. Islam prescribes prohibited degrees within which marriage is not lawful (4:23-25).

Above everything else, however, Islam is a religion, and is concerned not only with man's physical welfare in this life but also with his moral and spiritual welfare both here and Hereafter. It therefore adds certain regulations on the subject of marriage which are designed to serve as safeguards for the preservation and promotion of moral and spiritual values. These values are not the direct concern of the Declaration, but are the primary concern of religion, and to the degree to which a religion ignores or neglects them it ceases to fulfil its primary function.

The Unity of God is the central fundamental doctrine and concept which Islam teaches with insistence. Everything else stems from it and revolves around it. All order, all beneficence, all grace, all beauty, all health, all life, in short every positive value, proceeds from it and is dependent upon it. Were it otherwise, there would be no creation, no universe, no man; if any kind of existence could be assumed or imagined it would be all confusion, chaos and corruption. "If there had been in the heavens and the earth other gods beside Allah, then surely both would have been corrupted and ruined. Glorified then be Allah, the Lord of the Throne, above what they attribute" (21:23). "Allah has not taken unto Himself any son, nor is there any other god along with Him; in that case each god would have walked away with what he had created, and some of them would surely have dominated over others. Glorified be Allah above all that which they attribute to Him. Knower of the seen and of the unseen; exalted is He above all that which they attribute to Him" (23:92-93).

Associating anything with God, in His Being or in His atributes, is the gravest spiritual crime and malady. It might be described as spiritual leprosy: loathsome, incurable and unforgivable (4:49, 117), save through special Divine Mercy and Grace (7:157; 39:54).

If associating anything with God is spiritual leprosy, adultery is a foul moral disease (17:33). Marriage with a person afflicted with either of these maladies is prohibited (24:4). "Marry not women who associate anything with God until they believe, truly a believing bondswoman is better than a woman who associates others with God, although she may highly please you; and give not believing women in marriage to those who associate others with God until they believe, truly a believing bondsman is better than a man who associates others with God, althongh he may highly please you. These call to the Fire, while Allah invites to Heaven and to forgiveness that they may take heed" (2:222).

Those who profess allegiance to a religion but are in practice indifferent towards the values that the religion seeks, to inculcate, are a law unto themselves. They would chafe under all restraints and restrictions imposed by religion and would defy them, except where such defiance would arouse public opinion against them or would subject them to annoyance or unpleasantness. They are more anxious to stand well with men than to win the pleasure of their Maker. Their case is like that of those concerning whom it has been said: "Of a truth, they have greater fear of you in their hearts than of Allah. That is because they are a people who lack true understanding" (59:14).

But those who believe sincerely place spiritual values above everything else. For them it would be a very grave matter to submit these to an obvious hazard. In the case of marriage, a divergence between the parties on the question of religious allegiance might well constitute such a hazard, not so much on account of lack of tolerence or respect for each other's beliefs and practices could be presumed to have been settled and taken care of that his or her dearly loved and cherished life-partner should consummate the spiritual union between them by accepting and adhering to the same set of values in which he or she sincerely belives. The stronger the bond of affection between them, the keener would this takes the view that the wife is likely, in consequence, to be faced with greater difficulty than the husband. In the case of a non-Muslim woman contemplating marriage with a Muslim, it would be for her, in consultation with her parents, guardian or other adviser, to decide whether she should or should not place herself in that position. If she should be willing, it is lawful for the Muslim to marry her. "This day all good things have been made lawful for you. It is lawful for you to invite the People of the Book to eat with you and it is lawful for them to invite you to eat with them. Lawful for you are chaste believing women and chaste women from among those who were given the Book before you, when you give them their dowers, contracting valid marriage and not committing fornication nor taking secret paramours. Whoever rejects the faith, his work has doubtless come to nought, and in the Hereafter he will be among the losers" (5:6). From the point of view of Islam, if the wife, in such a case, became a Muslim, the change would be most beneficial for both and for the children, both here and Hereafter.

In the case of a Muslim woman, permission to marry a non-Muslim, even one believing in a revealed religion other than Islam, i.e. "from among those who are given the Book before you", has not been accorded. It would be better and wiser for her not to place herself in a position which would involve for her the risk of rejecting the faith and thus being among the losers in the Hereafter. The children of such a union, were it permitted, would be exposed to the same risk.

These are some of the limitations due to religion and neither the Declaration nor any piece of legislation can override them. If the Muslim woman concerned in the last case, for instance, refused her consent to marriage with a non-Muslim, there would be an end of the matter, for even the Declaration requires her full and free consent (Art. 16-2). If she were to consent but her guardian refused his consent, the marriage could still not take place under Islamic Law. She could not, in such a case, have recourse to the Qazi, for the guardian's refusal to consent would be in consonance with Islamic Law. If a form of marriage were gone through in such a case, it would be null and void under Islamic Law.

In certain jurisdictions such a marriage could be celebrated as a "civil marriage"; but this would, in most cases involve a declaration on the part of the woman that she has no religion, or at least that she is not a Muslim. Islamic Law would then cease to apply to her.

The attempt made in paragraph 1 of Article 16 to exclude the application of "any limitation due to ... religion" to the right to marry is also contradictory of Article 18, which is designed to safeguard, *inter alia*, the right of everyone "to manifest his religion or belief" in practice and observance.

Dissolution of marriage may be brought about by death or divorce.

On the death of the husband the widow is entitled to the payment of the unpaid portion, if any, of her dower, which ranks as a prior debt against the estate of the deceased, and to her share in the inheritance-one-quarter if the deceased has left no children, and one-eighth if there are children (4:13). She is also entitled to maintenance for one year in his residence (2:241). She is free to re-marry after the expiry of four months and ten days from the death of her husband (2:235); but should she be pregnant this period is prolonged, where needed, till she is delivered of the child.

Divorce is permissible, but is a long-drawn-out process. The basic concept is one of permanency of marriage. "Consort with them in kindness; if you dislike them it may be that you dislike something in which Allah has placed much good" (4:20). The Prophet's admonition to Zaid, quoted in the Quran, "Cleave to thy wife and be mindful of thy duty to Allah" (33:38) gives expression to the same concept. But differences may arise and incompatibility may threaten to make the union non-beneficent. Outside advice could perhaps indicate helpful adjustments and accommodations towards the restoration of harmony (4:36). Temporary separation might be tried, but the period should not exceed four months. If they should decide to resume relations, "Surely, Allah is Most Forgiving, Merciful" (2:227). But if nothing avails, and they decide upon divorce, "Then surely, Allah is All-Hearing, All-Knowing" (2:228).

But this is not the end of the chapter. There might still be room for cool reflection and a chance for remembered tenderness and beneficence to promote a reconciliation. Divorce should be pronounced twice at intervals of approximately one month. A resumption of relations at any time during this period would wipe out the pronouncement of divorce (2:230).

A divorced woman must wait for approximately three months (and if she is pregnant, till she is deliverd of the child) before she can remarry. "Their husbands have the greater right to take them back during that period, provided they desire reconciliation" (2:229).

When the end of the appointed period approaches the final decision must be taken to retain in a becoming manner or to send away in a becoming manner; "but retain them not wrongfully so that you may transgress. Whoso does that surely wrongs his own soul. Do not make a jest of the commandments of Allah, and remember the favour of Allah upon you and the Book and the 'Wisdom which He has sent down to you, whereby He exhorts you. Be mindful of your duty to Allah and remember that Allah knows all things well" (2:232).

If the decision should be a final parting "she would not be lawful for him thereafter, unless she marries another husband" and that marriage is also dissolved in due course, "then it shall be no sin on them to marry and to return to each other, provided they are sure that they would be able to observe the limits prescribed by Allah. These are the limits prescribed by Allah which He makes clear to the people who have knowledge" (2:231).

When the end of the waiting period has been reached and the divorce has become final, no obstacle should be placed in the way of the divorced woman marrying a person of her choice "when agreement has been properly reached between them. This is an admonition for him among you who believes in Allah and the Last Day. This is more beneficent for you and is purer; and Allah knows but you do not know" (2:233).

If it is desired and is agreed upon that a divorced mother should breast-feed her baby, the father shall make due provision for her maintenance, and the child shall not be made the cause for inflicting any suffering upon the mother or the father. "No soul is burdened beyond its capacity. . . Be always mindful of your duty to Allah and remember that Allah sees what you do" (2:234). In addition to all this there is the general exhortation: "For divorced women provision shall be made according to what is fair-an obligation on the God-fearing. Thus does Allah make His commandments clear to you that you may understand" (2:242-243).

Muslim jurisprudence has been very solicitous that while the welfare of a minor should be fully safeguarded and should be the primary factor in determining questions of guardianship and custody where they arise, due regard should be had to the claims and feelings of the parents in such cases. The Judge has a certain margin of discretion in every case, as circumstances may demand or indicate, but the general rule is that the guardianship of a minor (male or female) shall vest in the father, and failing him in the paternal grandfather, paternal uncles and male cousins in the paternal line in order of propinquity. But in the Muslim system of jurisprudence guardianship does not include the right to the custody of the minor. The right to the custody of a male up to the age of seven years and the custody of a female throughout minority vests in the mother, and failing her in the maternal grandmother maternal aunts and female cousins in the maternal line of propinquity.

This ensures that the general welfare of the minor and the claims of natural affection shall be suitably adjusted and harmonized. The minor's need for tenderness and affection during the most sensitive and impressionable period of its life is thus met.

This is a brief outline of the basic provisions of Islamic Law on the subject-matter of Article 16. These provisions aim at regulating the most important group of human relationships along beneficent lines. They accord due regard to the worth and dignity of the human person, the complementary character of the relationship between the sexes, and the demands of nature. They keep in view fairness and equity, which make the paths of daily life smooth, rather than aiming at some academic notions of equality divorced from actual practical needs, and ignoring the differentation wisely made by nature between the sexes, so that the Divine purpose may be fulfilled. At every step, each regulation is supplemented with the admonition, "Fear Allah and be mindful of your duty to Him", and the reminder, "Allah sees what you do". The system, taken as a whole, is balanced and adjusted. The parties, as human beings, have reciprocal rights and obligations, but the man, carrying heavier responsibilities in certain respects, is given in certain situations more of a say towards resolving them. This co-ordination is seen very clearly, for instance, in the distinction made between guardianship and custody of minors. The Quran, characteristically, sums up this patteren of checks and balances in the words: "They (women) have rights corresponding to the obligations upon them in equity, and men in certain respects enjoy a higher degree of authority" (2:229).

Article 17

Islam recognizes the individual's right to own property alone as well as in association with others, and accords it full protection. In this sphere also, the legal right of ownership and the moral obligation of beneficent use and disposal have been co-ordinated and adjusted. This appears sufficiently from the brief description of economic values in Islam set out earlier.

The right to receive adequate compensation for property acquired by the State or a public authority for a public purpose has always been given effect to.

No arbitrary seizure of property is permissible.

Articles 18-19

These articles are concerned to secure the freedom of thought, conscience, religion, opinion and expression, including the freedom to change one's religion and to manifest it in teaching, practice, worship and observance, and the freedom to seek, receive and impart information and ideas through any media and regardless of frontiers.

In essence every religion possesses a missionary character. It starts with an individual and seeks to persuade and convince others of its truth and of the beneficent nature of the values it propounds. It must, therefore, stand for freedom of conscience, including the freedom to change one's religion and the other freedoms mentioned in these Articles, which are all consequent upon freedom of conscience; otherwise it would create barriers in the path of its own objectives.

Some religions have set territorial or racial limits to participation in their communion, but Islam's message is universal. It brooks no such limitation and proclaims these freedoms unequivocally and emphatically. Claiming, like all religions, to be based on truth, it naturally warns, constantly and repeatedly, of the dire consequences, moral and spiritual, that would follow from the rejection or neglect of the values that it proclaims; but it leaves everyone free to make his or her choice. Belief is a matter of conscience and conscience cannot be compelled. A person might be forced to say that he believes, but he can by no manner of means be forced to believe. This truth is proclaimed by the Quran: "There shall be no compulsion in faith. Surely, guidance has become distinct from error; whosoever refuses to be led by those who transgress, and believes in Allah, has surely grasped a strong handle which knows no breaking. Allah is All-Hearing, All-Knowing" (2: 257). "Proclaim: It is the Truth from your Lord; where fore let him who will, believe, and let him who wi11 disbelieve" (18: 30). The Quran explains that it is only within the competence of God, the Almighty, to make a person believe, but even He does not force anyone to believe. He leaves everyone to exercise his or her reason and judgment. If He does that, it behoves no one else to try to force people to believe. "If thy Lord had enforced His will, surely, all who are on the earth would have believed together. Canst thou, then, force people to become believers?" (10-100). "Proclaim: O ye people, now has the truth come to you from your Lord. So whosoever follows the guidance, follows it, only for the good of his own soul, and whosoever errs, errs only to its loss. I am not appointed a keeper over you. Follow that which is revealed to thee and be steadfast until Allah pronounce His judgment. He is the best of Judges" (10: 109-110).

"Verily, We have revealed to thee the Book with truth for the good of mankind. So whoever follows guidance, follows it to the benefit of his own soul; and whoever goes astray, goes astray only to its detriment. Thou art not appointed a guardian over them" (39:42).

Attention is, of course, repeatedly drawn to the difference between belief and disbelief and to the moral and spiritual consequences of righteous action in contrast with evil conduct; but there is not the slightest reflection or implication that conscience may be forced or compelled. "The blind and the seeing are not equal; neither are those who believe and act righteously equal to those who work evil. Little is it that you reflect" (40:59).

"The blind and the seeing are not alike, nor the darkness and the light, nor the shade and the heat; nor alike are the spiritually alive and the spiritually dead. Allah causes him to hear whom He pleases; and thou canst not make those to hear who shut themselves up in graves. Thou art but a Warner" (35:20-24).

"Shall We treat those who believe and act righteously like those who act corruptly in the earth? Shall We treat the righteous like the wicked? This is a Book that We have revealed to thee, full of blessings, that they may reflect over its verses, and that those gifted with understanding may take heed" (38:29-30). "So turn aside from him who turns away from Our remembrance, and seeks nothing but the life of this world. That is the utmost limit of their knowledge. Verily, thy Lord knows best him who strays from His way, and He knows best him who follows guidance. To Allah belongs whatever is in the heavens and whatever is in the earth, that He may requite those who do evil for what they have wrought, and that He may reward with what is best those who do good" (53:30-32).

The Quran lays down directions with regard to the manner in which the message of Islam is to be conveyed to mankind. "Say, O Prophet: This is my way: I call unto Allah on the basis of sure knowledge, I and those who follow me" (12:109). He was commanded: "Call unto the way of thy Lord with wisdom and kindly exhortations, and reason with them in the way that is best. Surely thy Lord knows best him who has strayed from His way; and He knows best those who are rightly guided" (16:126). That command is an imperative for all Muslims.

Islam stands for complete sincerity in all relationships and insists on conformity of conduct to profession.

"O ye who believe, be mindful of your duty to Allah, and always say the straightforward word. Thereby will He bless your works for you and forgive you your defaults. Whoso obeys Allah and His Messenger, shall surely attain a mighty success" (33:71-72).

"O ye who believe, why do you say that which you do not? Most displeasing is it in the sight of Allah that you should say that which you do not" (61:3-4J.

Hypocrisy and insincerity are frequently condemned in the Quran in severe terms. "The hypocrites shall surely be in the lowest depth of the Fire, and thou shall find no helper for them, except those who repent and amend and hold fast to Allah and hold their faith sincerely for Allah alone. These are among the believers. Allah will soon bestow a great reward upon the believers" (4:46-47).

It follows that Islam requires a person to profess what he truly believes in, and not to profess belief in what he does not sincerely believe, nor continue to profess belief in that which he has ceased to believe in. Claiming to be the truth, it invites everyone to believe in its doctrines and to practise its teachings and does not encourage disbelief or a hypocritical profession of belief. Should anyone cease to believe in Islam, he does not thereby incur any legal penalty. From the point of view of Islam he abandons the path of peace, security, beneficence and progress, and puts his moral and spiritual welfare in jeopardy. In the Hereafter he will be among the losers. "Whoever rejects the faith his work has doubtless come to naught, and in the Hereafter he will be among the losers" (5:6). But in all matters of conscience his choice continues to be free. This follows from "There shall be no compulsion in faith" (2:257). If, along with his change of faith or in consequence of it, he indulges in activities which constitute an offence, he will render himself liable to punishment for the offence, in the same manner and to the same degree in which he would have been liable had he been guilty of the offence without any change of faith. In other words, apostacy, by itself, however condemnable is a spiritual offence and entails no temporal penalty. This is the essence of the freedom to change one's religion. The Quran is explicit on it.

He who turns his back on the truth having once recognized and accepted it, and persists in his rejection of it till death overtakes him and no opportunity is left open to him to retrace his steps and make amends, enters the Hereafter in a state of spiritual bankruptcy. "They will not stop fighting you until they turn you back from your faith, if they can. Whosoever from among you turns back from his faith and dies in a state of disbelief, it is such as he whose works shall be in vain in this world and the next" (2:218). As the context shows, this verse has reference to a state of war. If in that state a Muslim went over to the enemy and took up arms against the Muslims he would be guilty of treason whether a change of faith was or was not involved; though in the then conditions it would have been inconceivable that such a one would still profess being a Muslim.

In the same context is the assurance, "O ye who believe, whoso from among you turns back from his religion, should know that in his stead Allah will soon bring a people whom He will love and who will love Him, a people kindly and humbly inclined towards believers and firm and impervious towards disbelievers. They will strive in the cause of Allah and will not fear the reproach of a fault-finder. That is Allah's grace; He bestows it upon whomsoever He pleases. Allah is Bountiful, All-Knowing" (5:55). This was a comforting and consoling assurance against any desertion that the enemy might succeed in procuring during the course of the war.

Change of belief, unconnected with hostilities, is

looked upon in the same way. It does involve a grave penalty, the displeasure of Allah, worse than death in the eyes of a believer, but of no consequence in the estimation of one who has ceased to believe. No temporal penalty is attracted, if the change of belief has not led to the commission of an offence. "Those who believe, then disbelieve, then again believe, then disbelieve, and then go on increasing in disbelief, Allah will never forgive them nor will He guide them to the way" (4:138).

"Surely, those who disbelieve after they have believed and then go on increasing in disbelief, their repentance shall not be accepted, and they are the ones who have gone astray" (3:91).

The Jews in Medina were constantly devising stratagems to create trouble for and confusion among the Muslims. One of the devices contemplated by them is referred to in the following verse: "A party of the People of the Book say: Profess belief in that which has been revealed unto the believers, in the early part of the day, and proclaim disbelief in it in the latter part of the day, perchance this might induce them to return to disbelief" (3:73).

This is clear proof that change of faith entailed no temporal punishment. For if apostacy had been treated as a capital offence, as has been alleged, no such device as is mentioned in the verse could even have been contemplated, since the party having recourse to it, having proclaimed themselves believers in the morning, would on announcing their disbelief in the afternoon have been liable to be executed. According to their poor opinion of the quality of the faith of the Muslims, this would have struck terror into the hearts of the weaker and wavering Muslims, rather than served to induce them to follow the Jewish example.

On freedom of teaching, practice, worship and observance of religion, the following may be instructive and of interest:

"Surely, We sent down the Torah wherein was guidance and light. By it did the Prophets, who were obedient to Us, judge for the Jews, as did the godly persons and those learned in the Law; for they were required to preserve the Book of Allah, and because they were guardians over it. Therefore fear not men but fear Me; and barter not My signs for a paltry price. Whoso judges not by that which Allah has sent down, these it is who are the disbelievers. Therein We prescribed for them: A life for a life, an eye for an eye, a nose for a nose, an ear for an ear, a tooth for a tooth, and for other injuries equitable retaliation; and whoso waives the right thereto, it shall be an expiation for his sins. Whoso judges not by what Allah has sent down, these it is who are the wrongdoers .

"We caused Jesus, son of Mary, to follow in their footsteps, fulfilling that which was revealed before him in the Torah, and We gave him the Gospel which contained guidance and light, fulfilling that which was revealed before it in the Torah, and a guidance and an admonition for the God-fearing. Let the People of the Gospel judge according to what Allah has revealed therein, and whoso judges not by what Allah has revealed, these it is who are the rebellious" (5:45-48).

The Prophet permitted a Christian delegation from Najran to hold their service, in accordance with their rites, in his mosque at Medina, and they availed themselves of the permission.[72]

The Quran invites, indeed enjoins, reflection and the exercise of reason, understanding and judgment at every step. Failure to do so counts as a serious default for which an individual is accountable. It thus seeks to foster the development of these faculties and actively promotes freedom of thought, opinion and expression .

"In the creation of the heavens and the earth and in

[72] Zarqani IV, p. 41.

the alternation of the night and the day there are indeed Signs for those who possess understanding; those who remember Allah standing, sitting and lying on their sides and ponder over the creation of the heavens and the earth" (3:191-192).

"We sent Our Messengers with clear Signs and Scriptures, and We have sent down to thee the Reminder that thou mayest explain to mankind that which has been sent down to them, and that they may reflect" (16:45).

"Do they not reflect in their own minds? Allah has not created the heavens and the earth and all that is between the two but in accordance with the requirements of wisdom and for a fixed term. But many among men believe not in the meeting with their Lord" (30:9).

'This is a Book which We have revealed to thee, full of blessings, that they may reflect over its verses, and that those gifted with understanding may take heed" (38:30).

"These are illustrations that We set forth for mankind that they may reflect" (59:22).

From what has been said so far, it follows that everyone must be free to seek, receive and impart information and ideas through any media and regardless of frontiers. This is essential so that knowledge may be fostered and ignorance dispelled. "Shall those who know be equal to those who know not? Verily, only those endowed with understanding will take heed" (39:10).

The Prophet has said: "The seeking of knowledge is a duty laid upon every Muslim, man and woman".[73] He exhorted: "Go forth in search of knowledge to farthest Cathay".[74]

It is somewhat paradoxical, however, that while the Declaration sets forth the freedom "to seek, receive and impart information and ideas through any media and regardless of frontiers", it does not seek to promote the freedom of travel, without let or hindrance, across frontiers in search of knowledge, information and ideas-a freedom that mankind had enjoyed for centuries and which has been seriously hindered in the present generation, with the consequent restriction of a fruitful source of knowledge and understanding.

Article 20

This article is designed to secure the right of free peaceful association which is, in fact, consequent upon the right to freedom of thought, opinion and

[73] Ibn Maja I, Ch.:Dignity of the Learned.

[74] Baihiqi, on the authority of As-Sayuti I, under letter a, p. 37.

expression. The need for its specific formulation has arisen in consequence of certain political and economic developments in recent times. Paragraph 2 of the article has direct reference to political and economic systems in which membership of certain parties, groups or organisations is sought to be secured or promoted through compulsion or coercion.

Islam stands firmly and uncompromisingly on freedom of conscience. It does not seek to secure even belief in God, which is the principal concern of religion, through compulsion or coercion. Much less does it obstruct free association for the achievement of beneficent and lawful purposes through peaceful methods. Indeed, it encourages and even enjoins such association and co-operation, but forbids co-operation in sin and transgression, which obviously cannot be described as "peaceful".

"Co-operate with one another in the promotion of virtue and beneficence; but co-operate not with one another in fostering sin and transgression. Be mindful of your duty to Allah; surely, Allah is severe in retribution" (5:3).

Conspiracies are severely condemned; all association and conferring together must be for the promotion of beneficence. "O ye who believe, when you confer together in private, confer not for the commission of sin and transgression and disobedience to the Messenger, but confer for the promotion of virtue and beneficence, and be mindful of your duty to Allah unto Whom you shall be gathered. The holding of secret counsels for evil purposes proceeds from Satan, that he may cause sorrow to those who believe; but it cannot harm them in the least, except by Allah's leave. In Allah should the believers put their trust" (58:10-11).

Three types of associations and conferences are encouraged as desirable and beneficent, namely, "those that are charitable, promote welfare and strengthen peace. Whoso does that, seeking the pleasure of Allah, We shall soon bestow on him a great reward" (4:115).

Article 21

This article seeks to secure everyone's right to participate in the government of his country and to have equal access to public service in his country, and that the freely expressed will of the people shall be the basis of the authority of government.

In this context the basic Islamic concept is that sovereignty over the universe belongs to God, but that man, as God's vicegerent, is invested with authority in certain spheres, as a trust, in respect of the exercise of which he is answerable and accountable to God. The principle operates in every sphere of life. The Prophet said: "Every one of you is a steward, and is responsible and accountable for that which is committed into his care. The Sovereign is responsible and answerable for his people, every man is responsible and answerable for the members of his family, every woman is responsible and answerable for her home and children, and every servant is responsible and answerable for the property of his master that is in his charge".[75]

In the sphere of government and the conduct of public affairs the Quran lays down certain general directions which must be carried into effect, but leaves the method of carrying them into effect to be worked out according to the needs, demands and requirements of each situation. It begins by prescribing as a binding obligation that authority in public matters, which it describes as a trust, must be vested in the people best capable of exercizing it. "Verily, Allah commands you to entrust authority into the hands of those who are best fitted to discharge it, and that when you are called upon to judge between, or exercise authority over,

[75] Bukhari II, Sect.:Marriage, Ch.:Wife is a steward in her home.

the people, you must do so equitably and with justice. Surely, excellent is that with which Allah admonishes you. Allah is All-Hearing, All-Seeing" (4:59).

This shows that sovereignty, in this context, is vested in the people and they are admonished to commit its exercise into the hands of those who are best fitted to discharge its responsibilities. The obligation thus laid upon the people to choose their representatives wisely, is balanced by the corresponding obligation laid upon those who are entrusted with authority to exercise it justly and equitably. These two obligations, if duly discharged, would ensure good and beneficent administration of public affairs. The concluding portion of the verse implies that the Muslims might from time to time be tempted to depart from these two fundamental principles and to try other experiments; but they are warned that what Allah has admonished them with is alone the most excellent and the most beneficent method of discharging these responsibilities. Allah will watch over the process and will call to account those responsible in respect of any default committed by them.

Islam has not prescribed any particular method for the exercise of the franchise and has left the people free to adopt such method or system as in any particular situation may be deemed to be best fitted for the purpose laid down.

The State must carry out its responsibilities in consultation with the people directly or through their representatives, as the situation may demand (3:160). This is necessary for the purpose of keeping the administration in touch with the people and informed of their views, and also for the purpose of training the representatives of the people in the conduct of public affairs. The administration of public affairs through appropriate consultation of competent persons should be a characteristic of Muslim society. "Those who hearken to their Lord and observe Prayer, and whose affairs are determined by mutual consultation, and who spend out of whatsoever We have bestowed upon them (42:39).

On the part of the people, co-operation with, and obedience to, those set in authority and entrusted with the conduct of public affairs is placed in juxtaposition to the duty of obedience owed to Allah and to His Messenger. If any differences should develop they must be settled in accordance with the precepts laid down in the Quran and illustrated and expounded by the Prophet. "O ye who believe, obey Allah and obey His Messenger and those who are in authority among you.

If you differ in anything among youselves, refer it to Allah and His Messenger if you are believers in Allah and the Last Day. That is best and most commendable in the end" (4:60).

The Quran and its illustration and exposition by the Prophet must always rule.

Articles 22-28

This group of articles is directed towards securing a reasonable standard of living for everyone through proper education, appropriate and adequate training, availability of work, gainful employment, so that human personality may have full opportunities of development, human dignity be safeguarded and human life become progressively fuller, richer, healthier and happier. Most of these objectives are covered by the social and economic values sought to be inculcated and promoted by Islam, a brief summary of which has been set out earlier. The rest spell out these values in specific detail, the need having been manifested by current social and economic systems.

In Islam all these are part of a more comprehensive pattern which includes moral and spiritual values also, as is bound to be the case with any pattern of values sought to be inculcated and promoted by a religion. In fact Islam treats social and economic values as complementary to moral and spiritual ones, and that is why the former have been expounded in such detail and have been sought to be fostered as part of a comprehensive pattern.

For instance, though the Prophet chose to live not merely a simple but an austere life, he warned against extremes of privation as likely to affect a person's moral and spiritual evolution. "Safeguard yourselves against penury, for it might tend to push a person into disbelief". For the same reason he said: "There is no monasticism in Islam", basing himself upon the Quran (57:28).

Islam inculcates the acceptance of life and the beneficent use of all Divine bounties. "Who has forbidden the adornment of Allah which He has produced for His servants and the good things of His providing?" (7:33).

At the dawn of human history it was laid down that all men shall be entitled to food, clothing and shelter. "It is provided for thee that thou wilt not hunger therein, nor wilt thou be naked, and that thou wilt not thirst therein, nor wilt thou be exposed to the sun" (20:119-120). This was the beginning of human society.

Islam put into practice the first effective concept of the Welfare State. Within a few years of the organization of the first Islamic State, the provision of basic necessities for everyone was asssured. Not only was the State fully conscious of its duties in this regard, but individuals were also keen to perform their obligations towards the widow, the orphan, the needy, the captive, the debtor, the neighbour and the wayfarer. Long before the general diffusion of prosperity had reduced the need and multiplied the resources, public as well as private, available for meeting it, the Prophet's exhortations and his own example had so stimulated and sharpened the concept of human brotherhood among the Muslims that sharing their all, even in the midst of adversity, became an outstanding Muslim characteristic. The Prophet had suggested that in case of extreme necessity it would be well to follow the example of the Ash'ari tribe "who, when confronted with shortage of provisions, collect all they have and divide it equally among themselves. So, they are of me and I am of them".[76] The Quran bears witness that these exhortations were taken to heart by the Muslims. Of the Ansars of Medina and the early refugees settled in Medina it says: "Those who had established their homes in this city before the newcomers and had

---

[76] Bukhari II, Sect.:Oppression, Ch.:Sharing food.

accepted the Faith. love those who come to them for refuge, and find not in their breasts any desire for that which is bestowed upon the newcomers but prefer them to their own selves, even though poverty be their own lot. Whoso is rid of the covetousness of his own soul -it is these who will prosper" (59:10).

By the time of the Abbaside Khilafat there was scarcely anyone to be found in any city of the Muslim domains who was in need of, or was willing to accept, charity. This was symptomatic of the tremendous revolution that had already been achieved in all spheres of life - social, economic, intellectual, moral and spiritual. Science, art, learning and philosophy burgeoned forth and permeated every layer of society. History, poetry, song and fable all bear witness to it. This is proof that Islamic values, as set forth in the Quran and illustrated and expounded by the Prophet, had been put into effect and had borne rich and plentiful fruit.

The basic objectives of these articles were thus achieved to a high degree under the Islamic system in the conditions that prevailed thirteen centuries ago. Some of the specific details set out in the articles are designed to meet conditions and needs which have emerged and manifested themselves in recent times. The larger objectives are still the same and, as already shown, Islam is in full sympathy with them. If any of the means and methods set forth in these articles are found to be out of step with Islamic values social, economic, cultural, moral or spiritual-alternative means and methods, more in accord with those values, can be availed of for the purpose of achieving the agreed objectives.

Articles 29-30

Like most subjects affecting human personality, the subject of human rights has many facets. Freedom rightfully occupies a place in the forefront. Yet to ensure due freedom for everyone, the freedom of each must be curbed, restrained and regulated. As has been wisely observed, our only real freedom is the right to discipline our freedom.

The Declaration has not overlooked this aspect. These two articles take care of it. It is a truism that every right carries with it a corresponding duty. It is the due observance and discharge of the duty that fully safeguards the right.

It must be recognized that legislative, administrative and judicial checks and safeguards, essential as they are and scrupulously as they must be devised and maintained, can cover but a sector of the total field of human rights. Further, legal sanctions, however valuable in their reparatory and deterrent aspects, can come into operation only after a breach of obligation has occurred, comes to notice and can be established by relevant and admissible evidence. This means, first, that the whole field cannot be made subject to legal sanctions and secondly that the sector which may be covered cannot be completely and effectively safeguarded.

What is further needed is a lively consciousness of the unity of man and the inter-dependence of all in present-day conditions. That consciousness can be aroused at various levels and through the acceptance of a variety of concepts and values. The most effective and pervasive concept however, is that mankind-all men, without distinction of colour, creed or race- are the creatures of the One Living, Loving, Almighty, Merciful and Compassionate Creator to Whom the welfare of each is equally dear, to Whom all must return and to Whom all are accountable and responsible for their thoughts, designs, motives, actions and omissions. Unless that concept grips and inspires the hearts and souls of men, it is not possible to establish true brotherhood and equality between all grades and sections of mankind. Here we enter the province of religion.

True brotherhood can be established universally

only through firm faith in the Unity of the Creator. That faith alone has the power to make our approach to each fellow being, of whatever race, colour, creed, religion or language, one of eager friendship and deep devotion. Each one of us must rcognize every other as a creature and servant of the Lord of the universe Whom we acknowledge, accept and worship as our Creator and Maker, and to Whom the deepest devotion of our hearts and our truest allegiance are due. Through Him and for His sake we can readily and truly accept each human being as a comrade and brother, a fellow traveller on the same path, a fellow participant in the same glorious adventure which is the seeking in all things the will and pleasure of our Lord and Creator, Most Gracious, Ever Merciful. This is the only way in which the welfare of every one of our fellow beings can become a matter of as grave concern to us as our own.

We must remind ourselves of the admonition, so timely, once more: "Hold fast, all together, to the rope of Allah and be not divided, and remember the favour of Allah that He bestowed upon you, that you were enemies and He put love for each other in your hearts and you became as brethren. You were on the brink of a pit of fire and He rescued you therefrom. Thus does Allah expound His Signs to you that you may be guided". (3:104).

The unity of man derives directly from the Unity of the Creator. It is only by virtue of our relationship through God, the Creator and Maker of us all, that we can arrive at a true realization of our own unity. There are, of course, other bonds - blood relationship, common nationality, common ideals, common pursuits, devotion to a common cause, etc., and these bring about association, co-operation, sympathy and a sense of belonging-but while they tend to bring together, they can also divide individuals, groups and nations. None of them can be relied upon to promote, foster and cement unity in all situations and circumstances. It is only the reality and firmness of faith in a common Beneficent Creator that can unite and foster sympathy, love and devotion.

The consciousness of accountability both here and Hereafter, resulting from such faith, can ensure the due discharge of the duties and obligations that we owe to our fellow beings in all spheres of life. These, in turn, comprise all their rights and freedoms. If a fraction of the care and concern that we devote to obtaining recognition of and respect for what we claim as our rights could be transferred and devoted to the scrupulous discharge of the duties and obligations that we owe to our fellow beings, all human rights in every sphere of life would be fully safeguarded.

VI

Prevalent Attitudes Towards Human Rights Among Muslims

The Prophet said: "My generation is the best, then the succeeding one, then the one after that, and thereafter a decline will set in which will last a thousand years".[77] So it has proved. The decline in moral and spiritual values began as the Prophet had indicated, and as the neglect of these values proceeded it began to undermine other values also, as was inevitable. But the process was a gradual one and was slowed down by frequent regional revivals and efforts at reform. The revolution ushered in by Islam was so comprehensive, so all-pervading, so broad-based and went down so deep that even a prolonged period of decline did not make the ill results visible to an outside observer till more than half of it had

[77] Bukhari IV, Sect.: Ar-Raqaq, Ch.: On eschewing worldly splendour.

elapsed. Besides, when Islamic values were weakened and undermined at the centre, they were often revived and strengthened and furnished evidence of vigour in outlying parts of the vast Muslim domains. The Prophet had furnished the assurance: "Allah will raise up among my people, at the commencement of each century, one who will revive the Faith for them". Down the corridor of the centuries this succession of divinely inspired teachers and guides has served to keep the torch aloft and shining.

The values seriously affected during the period of decline were those which were most sensitive to exposure to case and comfort and to a high standard of living. A prolonged period of prosperity blunted the edge of the finer and more delicate moral and spiritual perceptions, though it also brought into relief those qualities the exercise of which was aided and facilitated by the ready availability of means and resources.

Various causes have been cited for the decline, but the root cause was the neglect of the Quran and the ignoring of the primacy of values that the Quran had sought to establish. "The Messenger will say: My Lord, my people indeed treated this Quran as a thing discarded" (25:31).

Articles 1-3

Nevertheless, those qualities which had been woven into the social and cultural pattern of Muslim society, and had become characteristic of it, numerous as they are, escaped serious injury and damage. Among these is the concept of human equality and brotherhood. There is no race or colour consciousness in Muslim society.

Article 4

Yet perhaps the most flagrant departure from the teachings of Islam and their spirit was in respect of slavery and the slave trade.

As has been explained, restriction of freedom-and that subject to safeguards which rendered it least irksome-was permitted only in the case of such prisoners of war, captured on the field of battle in a war made obligatory in the cause of freedom of conscience, who were not exchanged or ransomed, or set at liberty as a matter of grace (47:5), or could not obtain release in pursuance of a deed of manumission (24:34).

Raiding for the purpose of taking captives was prohibited (8:68). The Prophet said that a person who sold a free man into slavery would incur the severe displeasure of Allah and would be liable to condign chastisement.[78]

Under these regulations, once freedom of conscience was established and fighting for that purpose ceased to be obligatory, all such restrictions should have come to an end; but this is not what in fact happened. The institution of slavery became firmly established in certain parts of Muslim lands and the Arabs earned notoriety in slave raiding and slave driving.

Article 5

The penalty for theft has already been commented upon. Except in Saudi Arabia and in certain Arab Sheikhdoms it has given place to other forms of punishment.

Articles 6-11

The Quran set up strict standards of administration of justice, the independence and integrity of judges, non-discrimination, and the duty of witnesses to come forward to bear true witness without favour or partiality.

---

78 Bukhari II, Sect.:Hiring, Ch.:Withholding the wages of a worker.

But with the decline of other values, these standards also suffered decline. It is noteworthy, however, that the office of *Qazi* (judge) has throughout been held in high honour and enjoyed great prestige in Muslim lands.

Article 12

Muslim society has been particularly sensitive on the subject-matter of this article, and these values have throughout been sought to be safeguarded.

Articles 13-15

Islam has set up a world-wide brotherhood and a Muslim finds himself at home almost everywhere. As mentioned already, Muslims have been great voyagers. The idea of divided and separate nationalities is for them a comparatively new and somewhat unfamiliar concept, restrictive and sometimes disturbing in its manifestations, and irksome in practice. A Muslim is, by instinct and outlook, more of an Internationalist, or rather a world citizen, than a nationalist.

Arab nationalism, which began to be nurtured in the period immediately preceding the first World War, and received a great fillip during the course of that war and in the post-war period, is a recent phenomenon. The policies and rivalries of the Colonial powers, which did not fail to influence Turkey; the Middle East mandates, followed by the partition of Palestine and the setting up of the State of Israel, are some of the factors that have served to invest Arab nationalism with an aura of permanence. Even so, it is a linguistic, cultural and regional rather than a strict national concept.

Article 16

When a decline sets in in any society, the weaker elements, which stand in need of protection and safeguarding, suffer to a greater degree than the sturdier elements. Muslim society has been no exception. During its period of decline women suffered even more than men. Their position and interests were neglected and encroached upon, rather than supported and protected. They often became victims of man's greed, rapacity and passion, though outward forms were still sought to be preserved. Compliance with legal requirements, when they could not be circumvented with impunity, was often purely literal and sometimes served only as a cloak for deception and fraud. The spirit of equity and good conscience suffered a severe setback and men, instead of being watchful guardians over women and ever mindful of their duty to their Lord, became the exploiters of the fairer but weaker sex.

In the Islamic system woman, as an heir to her parents, husband and children and being entitled to a settlement as part of her marriage contract, could occupy a position of comparative economic security. She was often deprived of her rights of inheritance, the payment of her dower was neglected, and when paid it was in many cases appropriated by her guardian. So much did this become the norm in some sections of Muslim society that the dower began to be described by non-Muslim writers as the purchase price for the wife paid by the husband to her guardian. Educational standards deteriorated, again, more grievously among women than among men and, in consequence, among the poorer sections women often remained unaware of their legal rights and knew not how to secure and enforce them.

In the matter of the dissolution of marriage also, the position of women was seriously weakened. The safeguards provided by the Quranic jurisprudence were ignored, the moral injunctions were repudiated in practice, and even the letter of the law was whittled down to suit the caprice and convenience of the husband. The lengthy process of divorce, designed to provide frequent opportunities of reconciliation, was telescoped and the continuation of a marriage became dependent upon the sweet will and pleasure of the husband. The wife's right to demand a dissolution [khul'a] coextensive under the law with that of the husband, but requiring recourse to the Qazi so that the wife's position and property rights might be fully safeguarded-was permitted to fall into disuse.

The permission to marry more women than one at a time, subject to a maximum of four, designed to make provision for certain contingencies, was converted into a licence for self-indulgence. The strict condition of equality of treatment, "and should you be afraid that you may not be able to maintain equality between them, then marry only one" (4:4) was ignored altogether. The only restraint was imposed by the economic resources of the husband, and in many cases even this failed to operate.

Dissolution of marriage at the will of the husband, combined with the legal recognition of simultaneous marriages so long as the number of wives did not at any one time exceed four, brought the institution of marriage into contempt in certain areas and among certain sections of society, and served to divest it in a large measure of the sanctity with which Islam had sought to invest it.

Articles 18-19

Muslim society has striven throughout to uphold the values inculcated by Islam in respect of the promotion and fostering of knowledge learning and science. Indeed, it early set up a brilliant record in that respect. The Prophet said: "Allah will make the path of paradise easy for him who follows a track in the pursuit of knowledge; angels spread their wings for the seeker after knowledge; the dwellers of the heaven and earth pray for a scholar; a man of learning sheds more light than a worshipper even as the moon outshines other planets; the divines are the heirs of the Prophets and he who inherits their knowledge finds himself rich in all that is good".[79]

Among Muslims, knowledge has, fortunately, never been persecuted.

The same cannot be said of belief and doctrines. It is reassuring that the emphatic injunctions of the Quran on freedom of conscience were respected and obeyed so

[79] Tirmidhi II, Sect.: Knowledge, Ch.: Excellence of seeking knowledge.

far as they affected non-Muslims. But within Muslim society, departure from whatever happened to be current as approved orthodox doctrine was suppressed with the utmost rigour.

Persecution often proceeded to extreme limits. When bigotry donned the garb of politics, freedom of thought could be indulged in only at the risk of martyrdom. Some of the great Imams of juriprudence had to endure imprisonment and flogging for their refusal to subscribe to propositions which seemed to them erroneous or futile.

On one matter of fundamental importance the doctrinal position became crystallized in a manner directly contradictory to the express and clear declarations of the Quran.

While it continued to be recognized that in the face of the emphatic directions of the Quran on freedom of conscience, no one could be forced or coerced to believe, the dictum gradually developed that apostacy must be treated as a capital offence and punished as such. It was not appreciated that this involved a complete negation of the freedom of conscience repeatedly proclaimed by the Quran.

The confusion arose in this manner. After the Prophet was forced to leave Mecca and migrated to

Medina, where he was accepted as the chief executive by Muslim, non-Muslim and Jew alike, the Quraish of Mecca proclaimed a state of war between themselves and the Muslims which also involved the tribes in alliance with either side. This continued till the Truce of Hudaibiyyah brought about the cessation of hostilities. The Truce was broken by the Meccans in less than two years and hostilities were resumed on a much larger scale, followed rapidly by the fall of Mecca and by the Battle of Hunain, which broke the Arab tribal might and brought about the pacification of the greater part of the Peninsula.

On the death of the Prophet, several tribes which had submitted recently and reluctantly, raised the banner of revolt and advanced on Medina; and Abu Bakr, the First Khalifah, had to move against them.

In the meantime large-scale hostilities had developed between the Byzantine Empire in the north and the Muslims, and shortly after, in the time of 'Umar, the Second Khalifah, Iran also took up arms against the Muslims. It is understandable that the emergence so close to their borders of a republic based on freedom, equality and human dignity, which was rapidly gaining strength and influence and whose supposedly subversive ideas were spreading like wildfire, was most obnoxious to these two mighty empires based on privilege, and that they became most anxious to put an end as soon as possible to a phenomenon which threatened their very existence.

Thus the Muslims were successively and continuously forced, first by the Meccans, then by the tribes in different parts of the Arabian Peninsula, and finally by the two mighty Empires of Byzantium and Iran, to submit to the arbitrament of the sword.

After the fall of Mecca and the Battle of Hunain a large number of desert tribes, finding that the tide had set strongly in favour of the Muslims, declared their submission and announced that they had accepted the Faith, though most of them had yet acquired little appreciation of the values of Islam and possessed small comprehension of faith and belief. Concerning these, the Quran spoke as follows: "The Arabs of the desert say: We believe. Say to them: You have not believed yet, but say rather: We have submitted, for true belief has not yet entered into your hearts. If you obey Allah and His Messenger, He will not detract anything from your good deeds. Surely, Allah is Most Forgiving, Merciful. The believers are only those who truly believe in Allah and His Messenger, and then doubt not, but strive with their possessions and their persons in the cause of

Allah. It is they who are truthful.

"Say to them: Will you acquaint Allah with your faith, while Allah knows whatever is in the heavens and whatever is in the earth, and Allah knows all things full well? They think they have done thee a favour by their adhering to Islam. Tell them: Deem not your accepting Islam a favour unto me. On the contrary, Allah has bestowed a favour upon you in that He has guided you to the Faith, if you are truthful. Verily, Allah knows the secrets of the heavens and the earth. Allah sees all that you do" (49:15-19).

In these conditions of stress and turmoil, there were cases of defection of groups or of individuals. When an individual or a group defected from the Muslim side and went over to the enemy, they denounced Islam. These were cases of treason as well as of apostacy. In truth no real change of religion was involved. These people's declaration that they adhered to Islam was evidence of political submission rather than of faith on the basis of belief. When they changed sides they renounced political allegiance, became adherents of the enemy and joined its forces. They were described as apostates, a generic term which, in the conditions of those days, connoted the political crime of changing sides during the course of the war, made public and effective by a denunciation of Islam. In such cases, when those guilty became amenable to the jurisdiction of the Islamic State, they were liable to be punished for their treason; which offence, in the circumstances then prevailing, became synonymous with apostacy. Apostacy thus became a term interchangeable with treason. For instance, the tribes who marched against Medina after the death of the Prophet and against whom Abu Bakr had to take up arms, were ,in essence rebels, and yet they were also apostates and were so designated.

Apostacy having thus acquired a double connotation, the penalty for the political crime involved became attached, by an easy transition, to change of religion, even when, in later times, no question of treason to the State was involved. As one wrong often breeds another, the mishief, grave enough in itself as nullifying the provisions of the Quran on freedom of conscience, did not stop there. Orthodoxy, once entrenched in power, soon arrogated to itself the function of determining what a person should believe and what he should discard or denounce. The Prophet had said: "Honest and sincere differences of points of view among my people should be accounted a blessing".[80] Even these

[80] As-Sayuti.

began to be treated as objectionable innovations, were denounced as heresies and when, in the view of the favoured divines, they touched on matters which had been pronounced by them as essentials of belief, were condemned as apostacy involving the extreme penalty.

As already observed, this juridiction did not extend to non-Muslims. They were completely free to believe as they chose.

Article 21

The Quran had enjoined "Verily, Allah commands you" that administration should be carried on through the exercise of the franchice (4:59) and in consultation with the representatives of the people (3:160). It had warned that this was "the most excellent method" and should, therefore, not be departed from. But a shift towards monarchy started after the first four Khalifahs, and the Khilafat took on more and more the complexion and trappings of monarchy. Among the lines of Heads of State in Damascus and Baghdad, and later in Cordova. Granada, Fez, Cairo, Delhi, Istanbul and several other capitals, there followed a whole galaxy of brilliant, wise and beneficent rulers and administrators, simple, pious, devoted and God-fearing; they "enjoined equity and forbade iniquity" and proved themselves righteous servants of Allah. They illustrated in their lives and example the saying of the Prophet, "The Chief of a people is truly their servant".[81] Their annals illumine and adorn whole chapters and volumes of history. But the increasing disregard of the fundamentals laid down by the Quran, mentioned above, began to effect other values also and this could be perceived not only in the deteriorating standards of administration but also in the decline in the social, economic and intellectual spheres. Over wide regions freedom and independence were forfeited or mortgaged. It was a case of, "Then there came after them successors who neglected Prayer and followed evil desires. So they will meet with ruin" (19:60).

While, however, a neglect of the values taught by the Quran was bound to entail loss and damage in every sphere, a return to those values would revive beneficence, progress and prosperity for all in every direction. These values have been tried over long periods in vast regions of the earth by men of all races, colours and conditions, and have proved their total beneficence. "This is a perfect Book; there is nothing in it partaking

[81] As-Sayuti II, p. 29 under letter S.

of doubt or harm; it is a guidance for the righteous, who believe in the unseen and observe Prayer, and spend out of whatsoever We have bestowed on them; and who believe in that which has been revealed to thee, and that which was revealed before thee, and they have firm faith in what is yet to come. It is they who follow the guidance of their Lord and it is they who shall prosper" (2:3-6).

VII

Future Relationship between Islam and the Universal Declaration of Human Rights

The Declaration concerns itself only with certain aspects of human life and human relationships and must perforce seek to achieve its ideals through legislative, administrative and judicial safeguards and action. It cannot avail itself of the means and methods necessary for achieving a more comprehensive and far-reaching revolution in the lives of individuals and peoples. The purely moral and spiritual aspects of life, except in - so far as they are inevitably involved in all human conduct, are beyond its objectives. Nor does or can it concern itself with the Hereafter. Even subject to these limitations it constitutes an epoch-making formulation of human rights, based upon the widest possible consensus so far achieved and recorded.

Religion must travel far beyond the Declaration both in its objectives and in its methods. It is concerned with the totality of life, both here and Hereafter. The Declaration certainly, like Islam, claims universality and seeks that the rights, freedoms and duties set out and expounded in it should be accepted and made effective everywhere in respect of everyone. Thus in spirit the Declaration, so far as it goes, and Islam are in accord. In respect of certain specific details, the Declaration employs language which is too general; Islam spells out the necessary safeguards. Occasionally, but unavoidably, there is a difference of approach. Islam and the Declaration are both concerned with human welfare, prosperity and happiness; but while the Declaration is concerned to secure them at the material level, through physical means and during this life only, Islam being a religion, is concerned to secure them at all levels, through every available means, both here and Hereafter. Islam recognizes the inter-play and inter-action of all values and neglects none, but pays due regard to the need of co-ordination between them, which necessitates that a certain primacy must be assigned to and observed in respect of moral and spiritual values. These latter are not the primary concern of the Declaration. This divergence of approach leaves open the possibility of conflicting provisions for the regulation of a specific detail. Should this happen, and the conflict prove irreconcilable, then it is obvious that so far as Islamic society is concerned, the Islamic provision must continue to have priority.

Subject to this somewhat remote contingency, the revival and strengthening of true Islamic values would only help and further the achievement of the objectives of the Declaration.

As already indicated, Muslim thought, in all its aspects, has now been experiencing a healthy revival for close upon a century. The most helpful feature of this revival is that attention is being directed more and more to the Quran in the search for light and guidance in the fast-growing complexity of the conditions and values with which man is confronted today, and that the effort is proving abundantly, richly, extravagantly fruitful and rewarding. This is indeed in accord with the assurance contained in the Quran that its treasures of light and guidance are inexhaustible.

"Proclaim: If the ocean became ink for the words of my Lord, surely the ocean would be exhausted before the words of my Lord came to an end" (18:110).

And even more explicitly: "If all the trees that are

in the earth were to become pens, and the oceans were ink, with seven oceans swelling it thereafter, the words of Allah would not be exhausted. Surely, Allah is Mighty Wise'" (31:28).

These treasures will be preserved and safeguarded for future generations of mankind. "Verily, We Ourself have sent down this Exhortation, and most surely We will be its Guardian" (15:10). Thus the guidance set forth therein will continue to be available through the ages. If scholarship and reflection should fail to uncover it, it would be made manifest through inspiration and revelation.

The assurance conveyed by the Prophet, that Allah would continue to raise someone among his people at the beginning of each century who would revive the Faith for them, has been mentioned. There is an even more far reaching assurance in the Quran: "He it is Who has raised among the unletterd people a Messenger from among themselves who recites unto them His Signs, and purifies them and teaches them the Book and wisdom, though they had been before in manifest misguidance; and He will raise him among others of them who have not yet joined them. He is the Mighty, the Wise. That is Allah's grace; He bestows it on whom He pleases; and Allah is the Master of immense grace" (62:3-5).

This verse foretells a second spiritual advent of the Prophet in the person of one from among his followers whose functions would be similar to those of the Prophet himself. That prophecy was fulfilled in the person of Ahmad of Qadian (1835-1908), who set forth from the Quran the guidance needed by man in this age, when human life appears to be taking on new dimensions.

The Muslims are experiencing not merely a revival but a moral and spiritual resurrection. They are not all yet fully conscious of it; some are awake and alert, others are only half awake, but there is a stirring and striving and reaching out everywhere. A moral and spiritual revolution and rebirth brought about through revelation is described thus in the Quran: "Among His Signs is this, that thou seest the earth lying withered, but when We send down water on it, it stirs and swells with verdure. Surely, He Who quickens it can quicken the dead. Verily He has power over all things" (41:40). We are reminded of the same process elsewhere: "Thou seest the earth lifeless, but when We send down water thereon, it stirs and swells, and brings forth every kind of beauteous vegetation. That is because Allah is the Truth, and that it is He Who brings the dead to life, and that He has power over all things (22:6-7).

The "stirring and swelling" can be perceived through

the greater part of Muslim society, and already can be seen in places the sprouting of verdure and of beauteous vegetation.

The Muslims are becoming increasingly conscious of Islamic values in every sphere of life and are progressively realizing their beneficence. To the degree that this phenomenon spreads, grows and is strengthened, human rights will receive wider recognition and acceptance among Muslims and the values set forth in the Declaration will become more effective.

The progress so far made is most encouraging. The encrustations with which Islamic values have been overlaid through the course of centuries are being steadily scraped away, and the beneficence and true worth of those values are coming to light and are being restored and revived. This process is in operation at all levels and in every sphere - political, social, economic, moral and spiritual.

Systems of government are being overhauled. Absolute power is being checked and restrained and made progressively more responsive to the popular will. The latest instance goes so far as to disqualify members of the reigning family from holding office as Chief Justice of the Supreme Court, Prime Minister or Minister, or becoming members of Parliament. This is discrimination in reverse but has, no doubt, been considered necessary as a temporary safeguard to enable the newly framed constitution to work smoothly. The steady extension of the franchise is a healthy and welcome indication of movement in the right direction.

With the spread of education and a rise in the standard of living, the common man is coming into his own once more. As the decline had affected women more adversely even than men, the reverse process is proving even more beneficial for women than for men, though there is still a certain amount of leeway to be made up.

A note of caution must, however, be sounded. It is a homely but wise adage that all that glitters is not gold. In the social sphere, particularly, all that shines may not be beneficent. Islam aims at a joyous, cheerful, happy, but sober, restrained and responsible society. For this purpose it has devised a set of norms, adherence to the observance of which would safeguard society, as well as individuals, against all harm. Experience has proved their beneficence, it has also demonstrated the harm that follows upon their neglect. It would be wise to take both types of lesson to heart.

In the preceding section some comment has been offered on the deterioration of values in Muslim society in certain respects. A more hopeful note is called for with regard to the future, on the basis of the amelioration and progress that have already taken place.

The last vestiges of slavery are disappearing. It is devoutly to be hoped that that institution, with all its horrer and poignancy, will now be finally suppressed in those obscure corners where it still lingers and will be no more heard of.

Legal codes and judicial procedures have been and are being overhauled so as to eliminate all traces of privilege and discrimination where they may have crept in and to ensure speedy and equal justice for all. Civil and commercial codes have been modernized and improved in the light of experience gained in societies which have made rapid advances in commerce and industry.

In the sphere of Personal Law declaratory legislation has, in many Muslim States, cleared up doubtful points and obscurities in the effort to bring current doctrine into conformity with the standards prescribed by the Quran. On the subject of marriage and divorce, misinterpretations and abuse have been sought to be corrected. Registration of marriages and divorces has been prescribed; procedures for divorce have been clarified and the rights and obligations of the parties have been defined, thus placing them in a position of reciprocity.

Measures have also been adopted to give effect to the provisions of the law of inheritance, so as to safeguard the rights of female heirs and of orphans. Certain juristic anomalies have been corrected.

In the sphere of freedom of conscience, some degree of rigidity still prevails and a tendency towards fanaticism and persecution is noticeable among certain sections. As already explained, the practical result does not affect nonMuslims so seriously as it does Muslims who refuse to conform to what may be current as orthodox in a particular region. Few regimes would venture so far today as to exact penalties for such non-conformity, though the last case in which the extreme penalty was imposed occurred as recently as forty-three years ago; yet dissent is looked upon with suspicion and distrust, at best as eccentricity and, therefore, a nuisance, and at worst lunacy or criminal, and thus dangerous. Subtle methods of discrimination and persecution are resorted to, which operate to the prejudice and discomfort of the dissenter. Except in times of public excitement, when passion and prejudice take the upper hand and the more sober and reasonable elements prefer discretion as the better part of valour, there is little active violenlce. Paradoxically, certain democratic procedures, such as popular elections, have a tendency to incite the worst passions of the masses, and at such times recourse may be had to all sorts of devices to bring discredit upon unpopular institutions and individuals, especially the political or religious dissenter.

All this is regrettable and cannot be remedied by being merely swept under the carpet. The evil must be recognized, faced and striven against.

Fortunately, Muslim society has the remedy to hand. Difference or dissent, sincerely and honestly held, is no evil. The Prophet said:"Honest difference of opinion among my people should be accounted a blessing".[82]

The Quran is clear and emphatic: "There shall be no compulsion in religion. Surely, guidance has become distinct from error" (2:257). Even more clearly has it been announced: "The Truth is from your Lord; wherefore let him who will, believe and let him who will disbelieve" (18:30). ·"And who is more truthful in his word than Allah?" (4:88).

The conclusion of our discourse is: "All worthiness of praise belongs to Allah, the Lord of the worlds" (10:11).

[82] As-Sayuti.